YOU WANT TO BUILD AND FLY A WHAT?

OR... HOW I LEARNED TO FLY, BUILT A WWI REPLICA, AND STAYED MARRIED

BY DICK STARKS

Butterfield Press

Queries regarding rights and permissions should be
addressed to the publisher, Butterfield Press,
283 Carlo Drive, Goleta, CA 93117.
Phone: 805-964-8627. Fax: 805-964-8697.

Printed in the U.S.A. by Thomson-Shore, Dexter, MI.

Editing by Anne Leach.

Cover design by Quentin Eckman.

Second printing.

Acknowledgements

The ordeal you are preparing to undergo would not have been possible were it not for the efforts and inspiration of some very special people.

The inspiration came from Frank Kingston Smith, author of *Weekend Pilot*. His book started me thinking that maybe I could afford to learn to fly.

The efforts came from Virgil Vetter, the flight instructor who agreed, to his later dismay, to take me on as a student and teach me to fly.

Dave Martin, and Mary Jones, the editors of *Kitplanes*, and *The Experimenter*, respectively, encouraged me and egged me on to continue my exaggerations.

Judy Wood, editorial consultant, and Rusty Witter, writer and author, gave invaluable assistance and advice in writing the book.

My father, Burke Starks, an old-time, retired aircraft powerplant engineer, put up with ceaseless whining and complaining during each annual inspection. He never beat me over the head with a wrench when he had every reason to do so. I learned a lot from him.

Tom Glaeser — you'll read a lot about him — talked me into buying my first plane in 1979. Five years later he introduced me to homebuilt aircraft which opened yet another chapter in the wonderful world of aviation. I could never have done it without him.

A very special, humble note of thanks goes to Keith Connes and Anne Leach, the owners and operators of Butterfield Press. They were very supportive, patient and encouraging as they led me through the tortuous labyrinth of steps that constitute the publishing process. I'm sure that more than a few times, they were ready to chuck me and the book out the nearest window. They put up with a lot.

And last, but certainly not least, Sharon, my sweet, lovely, constantly suffering, patient, destined-for-sainthood wife. In the following pages, you will read my story about the long-awaited consummation of my love affair with flying. None of it would have been possible without the help and encouragement I received from Sharon.

Contents

III
The Dawn Patrol Flies Again

IV
More Aerial Adventures

Foreword

I wish I had written this book. I've been a pilot since 1957 and written the back page of *FLYING* magazine since 1970, read all the great aviation books and successfully stolen from most of them, but we are all just alike; "There I was, flat on my back, nothing on the clock but the maker's name, and..." and due only to the superior skills, iron nerve, super cool head, the pilot recovers and lives to tell the story. Yea, even sell it to a magazine.

As a matter of family tradition I always called home after each flight and I always said the same thing, "Once again we have cheated fate." I had gotten to where I believed my own stuff.

Then along comes Dick Starks, this bumbling Dagwood cartoon of a pilot. He bumbles, fumbles, stumbles at even the most simple tasks, yet lives. Worse than that he has the utter lack of shame to sit down and reveal it all in this book.

This book which will cause the veteran pilot to blush because somebody is at last telling it as a average human bean instead of a faultless hero, this book which in the paws of a novice, a new boy, a nugget, will cause a trickle of hope as he faces the solemn wall of wanting to fly his own airplane in the company of real pilots. "Golly, I could do that," says the groundling to himself after reading this book. Then goes out to the airport, gets a warm or frigid welcome as the case may be, and starts off as Starks did, learning the round end from the sharp end.

Dick Starks leaves out nothing. He not only tells of each experience but admits how he feels about it. He writes in plain words for those whose lips move while they read, and flicks away the last crumb of snobbery with a Glossary of Aviation Terms in the back that is so funny, warm and disarming that I would suggest you turn to the back and read that right after you finish these golden words.

Starks unsettled me a bit at first, calling his wife "Sweetums" and his airplane "Tweety Pie." Or was it the other way around. Hard for me to manage you see because I had taught my wife to call me "Ace."

I must also tell you that Starks lies.

For all his confessions of fear and humble bumbling, the man has a most direct thinking process, understands what he wants, goes for it without a lot of shilly-shallying, and is also a quick study. A careful reader should note that while he plays the fool in the book, Starks is an achiever, gets every rating he goes for and in minimum time. Starks never mentions anything like this but the facts reveal it.

The first lie from Starks is a whopper. After a bookload of trembling and gasping during which he also succinctly tells everything that happens to every student, both the problems and the solutions, he admits to being a World War One aviation buff who has actually lived out his fantasies by building a Nieuport 11 fighter plane and teaching himself to fly the feisty little single seat fighter. This airplane of about 1914 vintage is a true primitive, only about half a step beyond the experiments of the Wright brothers in America and Louis Bleriot in France.

Thus, halfway through the book, we discover that the quailing and quivering Dick has big ones of solid brass, for you could seat all the men who have ever done what he did in the cabin of a DC-3 and still have room for hot and cold running stewardii.

For this first book, the author stumbled around and somehow found Keith Connes of Butterfield Press as his publisher. No corporate office hound, Connes is a veteran and highly respected aviation writer and pilot. With all this going for him, they got Bob Stevens to illustrate the book. At this writing Starks and I have never met, but Stevens is an old and beloved friend. His puckish, wry, but gentle humor and authenticity from years of building a national reputation for cartooning for aviation publications and his own books is a most fortunate match here.

This book is a unique departure from the grim norm of aviation writing and at the same time a valuable preview of what to expect when at last you decide to come fly with us. Enjoy. Enjoy!

— Gordon Baxter

Introduction

This book was written for the other dreamers out there who always look up as a plane flies overhead.

If you're a non-pilot thinking of making the big jump into flying, reading this book should give you an inkling of the incredible adventures you can anticipate.

If you're a grizzled "spamcan" driver, this narrative might set you to thinking about expanding your horizons by jumping into the fascinating and challenging world of homebuilt aircraft. (If nothing else, reading the hangar tales in these pages will remind you of your own bull-slinging sessions with other prevaricating pilots.)

This book covers about a thirteen-year period and contains my more memorable escapades while learning to fly, buying my first plane, and building the next two.

One of my homebuilts, "Le Faucon Gris," is a replica of the famed Nieuport 11. The Nieuport was the first plane ever flown in combat by American pilots, the wild young men of the Lafayette Escadrille. There's nothing quite like having your own WWI fighter plane!

The second project, a Kolb Twinstar, is an ultralight. It was a lot easier to build than the Nieuport — and, being a two-seater, it allows me to take my wife Sharon along.

If you can walk and chew gun at the same time, you can probably learn to fly. If you're bored and need a new challenge, have a mind open to new and interesting concepts, and possess a craving for memorable happenings, pleasure flying can open a big window in your life.

Flying a small plane is an experience like no other. Once you try it, you'll probably be hooked for all time. The god-like feeling of accomplishment you get from a "perfect" approach and landing is immeasurable. On a smooth, crystal-clear morning when you can see forever, watching the sun come up from the cockpit of a small aircraft as you wend your way through the clouds is truly an emotional high.

I sincerely hope that if you are a non-pilot, reading this book will inspire you to rush to the phone and set up an appointment for your first flying lesson.

If you are already a pilot, my wish is that the feelings I express about my love for flight will touch a responsive chord.

—Dick Starks

I

How it all Began

I Start to Dream

"Take her around yourself and
see what it's like."

The empty runway stretched out green and ominous through the windshield in front of me. Heat waves rising off the baked grass caused it to shimmer surrealistically in the sultry, mind-numbing heat. The humidity was as it can be only in the Missouri River bottoms in early September. The cockpit was a close approximation of Hell as I sweltered miserably in it. It was like being in a loud, claustrophobic sauna. The Continental C-85 in my Cessna 120 was muttering impatiently as it idled, waiting for the idiot behind the throttle to do something besides sit there and sweat. The moment that I had dreamed about for my entire misspent life had arrived and I was scared speechless (or some other word to that effect).

I had been an aviation nut since I was old enough to look up when a plane flew over. For years, model airplanes in many different forms had been sufficient to satisfy my yearnings for wings, but no longer. I had searched for months for the plane that I now owned and was trembling in. Since starting flying lessons, I had known that I was going to have to solo sooner or later, but right at this time I would have preferred later.

I was inordinately proud of the 6.7 hours I had accumulated in my priceless student pilot's logbook and had figured that in about ten more hours I should be ready to solo. BUT NOT NOW!!! I figured out what my chances would be if I taxied back to the hangar and told Virgil, my instructor, that I didn't want to do it. That thought took about five seconds to discard, because I didn't think I would be able to take the look of disgust that would crease Virgil's face at my cowardice. As it was, the yellow streak that runs down my back was rapidly expanding and was about to meet at my belly button. Besides that, Virgil might just leave me at the airport and fly off. I had to do it!

My feet were dancing on the rudder pedals and my heart thundered in time with the idling engine. I blinked the sweat out of my eyes and wiped my hands once more on my already soggy pants. It seems that at least once a year I get in a position to ask myself, "HOW DID YOU EVER GET IN THIS MESS?" Well, here we were again. I embraced the fear and panic like two old friends.

* * *

At least, this latest disaster in my life had taken a long time to arrive at its climax. As usual, it was all Tom Glaeser's fault. Tom and I had been getting into trouble together since our high school days. We chased the same girls, and Tom, for awhile, in spite of all my warning about what she was really like, dated my sister. We worked on junker cars together, built and raced sailboats together, and both got involved in airplanes at an early age. We used to fly U-Control combat in my back yard and coined the term "instant kits" to describe what most of the flights looked like. We very rarely cut the other plane's ribbon. Usually it was a massive, sudden, and very entertaining mid-air collision. Sometimes it took several minutes for all the parts to flutter to the ground.

People used to come from miles around when they heard that Tom and I were going to be flying combat, just to see the crashes. We never disappointed them. We could build a plane in an evening — and we put in a lot of evenings surrounded by the smell of butyrate dope and glue.

When we both finally got our first summer jobs, the sudden influx of new funds made it possible for us to get into radio control airplanes. Now the crashes meant that a lot more money had just smashed into the ground. The craters were larger and the wreckage had interesting little electronic bits scattered in them to add color and variety. Our crowds of followers got bigger.

When we graduated from high school, we drifted apart for a few years. I went to college to get my teaching degree and he went to trade school to become a tool-and-die/injection mold/machinist/millwright specialist. The Vietnam years added to the separation. He got called up as a helicopter crew chief and I was teaching math. When we finally got back together, he was a machinist at TWA and had his pilot's license and I was getting fat. It was time to get in trouble again. He knew just what I needed.

When I heard that Tom had a pilot's license I started to think about getting one for myself. But if he hadn't invited me over to see his KR-2 homebuilt airplane project, I probably would have been content to keep on flying radio control models and spending my extra money on wild parties and high living. It took four years for the transformation from model builder to pilot to take place. It started with Tom giving me some old copies of *Trade-A-Plane** to look at.

Wow! What a revelation that was! I had thought planes were *expensive*. Well, at least they weren't terribly, *horribly* expensive. I mean, some of the ones in the paper were less than five figures.

One trip through the magic yellow pages of the pilot's wish book was all it took to get the juices flowing. By golly, some of those suckers could almost be afforded!

I started to dream and scheme. Sweetums (Sharon) had to be approached with care when something like this was in the works. She has abnormally acute extrasensory avoidance radar when it comes to spending money on "stupid things." I was sure that an airplane would be at the top of the "stupid" list.

When I asked her if it was all right if I took flying lessons she said yes. Then, I just casually mentioned about how much I was going to have to pay to rent a plane for the lessons. She got *that look*. Then, with an ease born from years of practice, smoothly and subtly, without a ripple, I laid it on. I've had years and years of practice. You've just got to know how to handle women — LIE! Or if you can't bring yourself to lie, AVOID THE TRUTH!!!

"You know, dear," I said with my best bland, innocent expression, "if I could find a good used plane for sale, I could buy it, learn to fly in

---

* *Trade-A-Plane* is the tabloid yellow-paged listing of planes for sale. It is published in Crossville, Tennessee and is probably the best publication to peruse when shopping for a used plane. Not only will you read of a lot of planes for sale, you can get very good ideas of the current asking prices of used aircraft.

it, and then sell it and not have spent a cent except for the instructor and gas. The plane is bound to appreciate in value while I have it and all that money would just be an INVESTMENT. Why, my dear, we could get it back in a second and maybe even make a tidy little profit." The lie slipped smoothly into place without making a ripple.

I waited with a thudding heart and bated breath for her response. I could see her mentally trying to figure all the different ways I was going to snooker her on this deal. Then, SHE SAID YES! Wow! The way was clear. A check for a subscription to *Trade-A-Plane* was in the mail the next day.

* * *

I started to look for my dream plane. I didn't know at that time that Tom had already figured out what kind of plane he wanted me to buy. As usual, I just went along with the flow and tried to make the best of it. It wasn't long before I was haunting all the small airports within a 50-mile radius of Kansas City, looking for just the perfect bargain. Boy, did I meet some fast talkers and smooth dealers. Since I didn't know anything about planes and Tom is an A & P (Airframe and Powerplant mechanic, licensed by the FAA), he soon started going with me to protect me from fast talkers (a weakness), pretty, big-busted sales-women (another weakness), and pretty paint jobs that covered a lot of unseen aeronautical sins (the biggest weakness). He really saved me from making some disastrous mistakes several times.

NOTE: I think I need to stop for a minute and define an aviation related term for you who are thinking of getting into flying or purchasing a plane to learn to fly in. It will also help to demonstrate how your local A & P will make himself verrry useful.

AD means Airworthiness Directive. It is probably the most horrifying term an aircraft owner on a budget can hear. I was to quickly learn (to my wallet's dismay and outraged screams from Sweetums) just what an AD was. Every time I get an AD from the FAA, I am convinced that an airplane is a direct open door to a black hole in the universe that vacuums up money like a goose sucks up corn. Sweetums would get a strained look around her mouth whenever I said, "You know, dear, there is a new AD out on Tweety and the plane needs...." I usually didn't get much more said. She makes Godzilla look like a pussy cat when she lights off her afterburners. Man, when that woman is MAD, she's nine feet tall and completely covered with hair. Sometimes I barely make the door. I can still hear her voice echoing around the neighborhood as I galloped frantically down the street. "INVEST-MENT! INVESTMENT??? INVESTMENT MY AUNT MARY! COME BACK HERE YOU BIG BLOCKHEAD!! I'LL GIVE YOU INVESTMENT!!!"

Anyway, back to the story. An AD is usually a little letter you get from the FAA telling you that there is something in your plane or engine that has been found to be defective and could effect its airworthiness. (In other words, a plane has either crashed or had an engine failure due to this whatever-it-is breaking or falling off.) You are directed to fix it or ground your plane. Hence, Airworthiness Directive. The kicker is that YOU, the owner of the plane, have to pay for the repair or replacement.

You know, if a company puts something out that later on turns out to be defective, doesn't it seem natural and good business that the company should pay for the new part rather than the poor slob who bought it? Not so in the aircraft world. Brother, if you are thinking of buying a plane, have an experienced A & P mechanic along to protect you and read the logbooks. If that plane has Bendix magnetos, then look twice. There were three ADs on them that didn't show up until after I had bought the plane and that was a $350 surprise at the first annual. (That's another thing I had to hide from Sweetums.) I have nothing against ADs; it's kind of nice knowing that someone is out there looking after us. It's just the way they are done from a pocket-book point of view. You can get a list of the ADs on a particular aircraft from the FAA and it could save you a lot of $$$$$s later on.

Now back to my search. Not only did I want a plane, I wanted a "macho" plane. I wanted a plane that I could swagger up to on the flight line to the envious looks of other pilots. I was going to be the fighter pilot of the Geritol set.

I firmly decided that the plane I bought would have to be a taildrag-ger — a plane whose landing gear configuration has two main wheels under the cabin and a small steerable wheel back by the rudder. Taildraggers are trickier to handle on the ground, hence the boast: "Real Pilots Fly Taildraggers." The more modern tricycle-geared aircraft have the third wheel under the nose, providing better visibility and handling on the ground.

Just hearing other pilots talk about taildraggers made me sure that

I wanted one. They have an aura and a mystique that I really admired. What I really wanted was a Cessna 120 or 140, a Luscombe or a Taylorcraft. These are two-place high-wing aircraft. The main difference between a Cessna 120 and a 140 is that the 140 is equipped with flaps.

I had read Frank Kingston Smith's book, *Weekend Pilot*, until the pages were ragged and stained with drool. His love affair with the 140 was infectious and I wanted one. It was at the top of my list.

The Luscombe was a close second to the Cessna because of its deadly reputation as a ground-looping son-of-a-gun. I read a story by a Luscombe pilot about how the plane would sit there reared back on its gear and look at you with slitted eyes and a sneer on its lips as you approached it. "Come on, sucker," it seemed to be saying, "MAKE MY DAY."

Taylorcrafts are great planes, too, and were high on my list at first, but I didn't have to look very long at them before I got the message. They were all either basket cases or immaculate restorations. The basket cases didn't interest me and the show planes were beyond my budget.

Aeronca Champs and Chiefs, on the other hand, are big-bellied puppy dogs that seem to waggle their tails with pleasure when you walk up to them for a flight. "Let's go have fun," they seemed to say. Every one of them I looked at was in the same category as the Taylorcrafts, either a raddled old lady of the skies needing a lot of TLC, or a sparkling debutante with an enormous price tag.

The classic Piper J-3 was out of the question. Take a look at a *Trade-A-Plane* and you will see why. They must be made out of gold tubes and fabric. (Well, they *are* yellow.)

The Cessna 120/140 is a sort of compromise between highs and lows of the group. She smiles at you like an attractive woman when you walk up to her but gives just a hint of warning that she will bite you if you let her get the upper hand. She's all metal (except for fabric-covered wings on earlier models) and parts can be found through Univair and J.W. Duff Co. I started looking for a 120 or 140.

About two months later I was about to give up. I was starting to look at 150s. They were all over the place in 1979 at decent prices. (NOTE: Not any more. Even those babies are getting expensive.) They weren't the "macho" plane I wanted but there weren't any 120s or

Luscombes out there that I could afford. Even Sweetums had relented from seeing me moping around the house with my boo-boo lip sticking out, and added another thousand bucks to the dream plane budget. That didn't help either.

Then I saw an ad in *Trade-A-Plane* for a Cessna 150 in the Kansas City area for a decent price. Low time, radio, and affordable. Who could ask for anything more? Tom and I went out to the airport.

You've got to be devious when you are shopping for a plane. If you come up in a cloud of dust to the plane with bugged-out eyes, your tongue hanging out, and your checkbook in your hand, you can probably forget any dickering and haggling over price. Tom and I had learned to park off the airport and saunter in with a poor and wistful look on our faces. No one will talk to you then. The pilots will be friendly but the salesmen will stay away from you.

We arrived at the airport and started looking for the plane. There was a pretty blue and white 150 parked out on the ramp and two guys working feverishly on it. We hid behind a hangar and watched them. They changed the oil, cleaned the plugs and then started her up. There was a cloud of smoke and a lot of backfiring. We skulked up behind a Cherokee to get nearer. Upon closer inspection, the 150 didn't look so impressive. There was hangar rash—the aviation equivalent of door dings on a car—on the ailerons and tail feathers. The wings and tail had been through one hell of a hail storm, too. My hopes started to plummet. Tom looked at me with my face drooping lower than a basset hound's and said we might as well go home.

Then it happened. Call it fate, Kismet, trapped gas, or chance. We decided to walk down a row of planes to the office to get a soda pop. We passed by a forlorn looking little Cessna 120 with flat tires, faded and peeling paint and a thoroughly sad and neglected look. The sign in the window told it all: FOR SALE. Tom stopped, looked, and walked over to her. He read the stuff on the sign and started to peek and poke around the plane. I stood there shifting from one foot to the other waiting for him to finish so we could go on. I was depressed and wanted to go home and sulk. "Come on, Tom," I said. "That thing's just waiting for the salvage man to come claim it. I want to go home and look at *Trade-A-Plane*." He kept on poking and prodding the plane. "Why is he spending so much time on that worthless hulk?" I kept

"Come on, Tom...that thing's just waiting for the salvage man."

thinking to myself. He even laid on his back under the fuselage and seemed to be studying something.

"Hey Dick," he yelled, "Come on over here. We don't have to look any longer. I've found your plane."

Incredulous, I walked over to the wreck. She was a mess. Duct tape was covering holes in the wing fabric, and there was so much ringworm and peeling dope on the wings that they looked fuzzy.

"You're out of your simple little one-cell mind," I told Tom. "I don't want a rebuild project!"

He wouldn't listen and dragged me to the airport office to get more information about the plane. The price was $4500. That was within my budget with room to spare; however, I wasn't prepared to buy a basket case and rebuild it. Tom sat me down and laid the facts on me. He started out by cussing to get my attention, and then began to talk.

"Look, Dummy," he gently said. "There's nothing wrong with that plane. The fuselage is straight, which means it probably hasn't had any *bad* ground loops.* I'm not saying that the plane hasn't been ground looped; there are only two types of taildraggers, those that have been ground looped and those that are going to be.

"And there's no hangar rash. The engine is clean and there's no surface corrosion that I can see. Everything you are upset about is cosmetic and can be easily fixed. Now, get up there and call the owner or I won't help you look at any more planes. I want to go over the logbooks."

When he talks like that I usually listen.

I called the owner. It was a familiar tale. He just didn't have the time to fly or care for her anymore. I got him to come out to the airport. While Tom was looking at the logs, I followed the owner out to the plane to get it ready for a flight. We pumped up the tires, changed the dead battery, and got in the plane. He started her up and we taxied out for a short flight. The booming in the back of the fuselage as we taxied along (the hollow metal fuselage acts as a megaphone, amplifying noise from the tailwheel) was echoed by my thudding heart. The takeoff was short and sweet. She might have looked like hell but she sure did seem to fly great. I started to dream.

---

* A ground loop is what happens, usually in a taildragger aircraft, when you lose directional control while landing. The plane spins around on one wheel and often digs a wing tip into the ground.

Twenty minutes later he greased her in with a perfect wheel landing. (With a Cessna's spring steel gear, that's a real feat.) After the landing he turned to me and said, "You want to taxi her in?" (In retrospect, I know he was just ensuring the sale; at the time it seemed like all my Christmas presents and steamy back seat adventures rolled into one.) We slowly wove our way back to the tie-down area, leaving a trail that a snake couldn't follow, and parked the plane. I already had stars in my eyes and was having trouble breathing. Tom dragged me off to the side while the plane was being tied down. "The logs look good and all the important airframe ADs have been done on the plane."

Tom told me to offer him $4000 and then split the difference when he refused my first offer. I was ready to hand over my life savings and throw in my first-born, but I followed Tom's directions. Tom is known over a four-state area for his rudeness and ruthlessness when dickering with car salesmen. Marine boot camp sergeants would pay tuition to be able to take lessons from him on giving abuse. Tom can cuss for five minutes and never repeat himself — a real master of his trade. I've gone car hunting with him a few times and I'm surprised he hasn't been shot.

I, on the other hand, am a pushover for any salesman. I generally buy the Girl Scout's complete cookie inventory. When my students get a form to fill out for a walk-a-thon, bike-a-thon, swim-a-thon, spell-a-thon or anything-a-thon I am the first one they always hit because they know a congenital sucker when they see one.

I casually offered the owner $4000 and held my breath. I almost fainted when he accepted the offer. I wrote out a deposit with shaking hands and SHE WAS MINE. I don't remember driving home. I do remember Tom coaching me on how to tell Sweetums and my parents that I had bought a wreck with wings. "You've got to pick just the right time," he counseled. He also said to have a clear line of retreat laid out with the door propped open and ready.

When I approached Sweetums, she was covered with flour and up to her elbows in dough with her nose in a cookbook. It was as safe as it was going to get. I took a deep breath and dug my toes into the floor as I poised myself for a quick getaway. The mixer was whirring busily and I knew from experience that she would at least take the time to turn it off before starting her pursuit. That would give me some lead-off time.

"Sharon, I bought a plane today."

She just absentmindedly nodded her head. "That's nice, dear. Take out the garbage." She never looked up. One hurdle down, one to go.

With my parents, I had to be more subtle. I waited until both of them were in bed to call and tell them so they wouldn't fall too far. My dad is an old A & P from back in the 30's and 40's, so he took it a lot better than my mom. She could already see me as a smoking crater in the ground. My dad said that I couldn't even start up the engine until he had taken a good look at the plane. Since that was my intention all along, I gave in gracefully.

When he first saw the plane, he almost had a coronary. I thought he was going to shoot me. However, after he had inspected her from spinner to tailwheel, he agreed with Tom. It was a good, solid airplane that needed a little tender love and care.

The next week was spent getting hangar space at a nearby little airport, Noah's Ark International (which is in the southwest portion of the Kansas City TCA* and a delightful little grassroots airport) and finishing the financial details of the sale. I was lucky on both counts. The plane was ferried to Noah's and the final papers signed.

* * *

Now I had to find an instructor who understood taildraggers. I called six different guys who had told me they would teach me to fly. When I told them I had bought a 1946 Cessna 120, they all backed water and told me they didn't teach taildragger. I was sort of lost as to what to do next.

Then fate stepped in again. We were just parking the plane in her new hangar space when Noah Dunnagin, the owner of the airport, told me to go talk to a guy who was taxiing in from giving a lesson. He was Virgil Vetter, a CFI who flies the prettiest, shiniest 1946 Swift that you will ever see.

Virgil is a very good-looking, silver-haired, very quiet, soft-spoken guy who can make a plane sit up and talk.

I walked up to him and said, "Hi. My name is Dick Starks."

As he tied a wing down he slowly looked me up and down.

---

* Terminal Control Area—airspace surrounding a major airport that cannot be entered without a clearance from air traffic control. Effective September 16, 1993, it will be renamed "Class B Airspace."

"I just bought that Cessna 120 over there and I need a taildragger flight instructor to teach me to fly." I held my breath, waiting.

There was another long silence.

"So, you want to learn to fly?" he said.

"Yeah. Will you take me on as a student?" Inside, I was saying, "PLEASE! PLEASE! PLEASE! PLEASE! SAY YES!!"

I am sure that he didn't have the slightest idea of what he was getting into, but he said, "Yeah, I suppose." Such enthusiasm! I set it up with Virgil to take three lessons a week. My first lesson was to be on August 18, 1979.

I was set to go. I had a plane, hangar space, and an instructor. The moment I had been longing for all my life was at hand. I ran out and got examined for a third class medical certificate. (How's that for stupidity: I bought the plane before I knew if I was going to be deemed healthy enough to fly it.)

* * *

It was time for my first lesson. Dad and I had gone over the plane for a week, checking everything out. The only things he had me do were patch the holes in the wings with dope and fabric, clean the plugs, put in a new battery, and check the timing on the mags. SHE WAS READY!!! She still looked like hell, but the important stuff was first class!

I showed up two hours early for the lesson. After six or seven preflights I sat in her, working the controls and making motor noises with my lips. In my mind I was performing beautiful coordinated turns and greaser wheel landings where the wheels kissed the runway with a quiet chirp, chirp.

I did this until Virgil showed up. For about thirty minutes, he discussed in detail what we were going to do both on the ground and in the air. This included a preflight inspection. He solemnly informed me that "Every safe pilot always does a preflight." I learned how to check the oil, check the tires, check the fuel for water or other contaminants, check every control surface and all the other little things that need to be eyeballed before flight. Then we got in the plane.

I taxied down to the end of the runway at a speed so slow that Virgil had time to grow a few more gray hairs. Then he talked me through the magneto checks, altimeter setting, control check, carburetor heat check, and we finished the pre-takeoff checklist.

I got ready for him to take her off. He looked over at me and said, "Keep her straight on the runway and she'll take off by herself when she wants to." Oh God! I said to myself. I'm not ready for this.

I shoved the throttle in all the way. The engine bellowed and we started to thunder down the narrow asphalt ribbon. I could feel Virgil correcting my terrible rudder action to keep her on the runway. As we rocketed by the airport office, I saw money changing hands as the locals laid bets on how long I would last before Virgil told me I was untrainable.

That first lesson was a real revelation. I saw then why Virgil said that most of our lessons would only be about an hour long. After about 45 minutes my brain was hanging limp between my ears. There was so much to remember and do. I would never be able to learn all this stuff.

When it was over I was wondering what in blazes I had done to myself this time. (I seem to ask myself that question a lot.) I couldn't taxi in a straight line to save my soul, a statue would get nauseous from my control movements, and I was bewildered and lost when we were five minutes away from the airport. I thought all those years of radio control flying would make me a master of the controls and the letdown was depressing.

I resolved to do better. That night I went to a bookstore and bought William Kershner's "Student Pilot's Flight Manual" and the FAA question book for the written exam. (If you are looking for a study guide, Kershner's books are the best ones to buy. He writes with a sense of humor and is easy to read and understand.)

Like I said, Virgil is a very quiet and soft-spoken person. When I called him on the phone to arrange a lesson or ask some questions, the conversations were usually short and one-sided. The phone would be picked up and Virgil would say "H'lo."

"HEY VIRGIL, THIS IS DICK!" I would yell over the phone.

"Hey, what's going on?" he would reply. Then by golly, I had better have something important to tell him or the whole phone call would be wasted. There would be these long hollow silences as I tried to think of what to say. This was a new experience for me. Tom and I both blabber to each other at the same time, neither of us listening to what the other is saying, and both of us having a hell of a good time. With Virgil, I had to change my phone conversation habits. We would finally set a time for the next lesson and the one-sided conversation would end.

I always tried to get to the airport an hour early so I could do a super-duper preflight and get in a little Walter Mitty cockpit-sitting while waiting for him to arrive. When he would skillfully grease his Swift onto the runway, my jaw would gape in amazement and envy. How did he do that? I could never get that good.

We would spend about ten minutes on the ground where he would tell me exactly what was going to happen and what he expected me to do. Then we would get into the steamy little cockpit, thrash out to the west, and start to work.

A flying lesson with Virgil was a very entertaining and educational experience. Virgil would tell me what to do, watch me do it, give a big breathy sigh and tell me to get on the controls and follow him through the maneuver. Then I would try it again. Over and over, over and over till I finally got it right. Then we would go on to something else. Then we'd come back to the first maneuvers.

As I got better and better he would spend more time just telling me what I was doing wrong and tell me to do it again. He got so he would only grab the controls when I screwed up really bad. He never yelled or thumped me on the head, even though he had plenty of reasons to do so. Sometimes I could never seem to get it right. He would just sit there with his arms folded, a disgusted look on his face, and slowly shake his head. When he did that, I felt like I was hurting his feelings by doing so badly. So, I would try harder and — of course — do much worse. Finally Virgil would sigh and say, "I think you've had enough today. Let's go back to the barn." Another educational disaster would be history.

Gradually, as time and lessons wore on, a sequence of events would evolve in the cockpit. Virgil would sit there with his arms folded and his feet on the floor plates and tell me what he wanted me to do. If I was doing well, his arms would stay folded and he wouldn't say anything except to tell me how I could improve what I had just done or what he wanted me to do next. I'd be right in the middle of whatever it was that he was wanting me to do and suddenly a thrill of horror would run through my body. Out of the corner of my eye I could see HIS ARMS WERE SLOWLY STARTING TO UNFOLD! What was I doing wrong? I'd frantically start to push and pull the yoke to try and fix whatever mistake I was making. If his arms slowly folded back up I would heave a sigh of relief and go on. If what I did was making things worse, the arms would slowly unfold even more until his hands were on his knees just out of reach of the madly gyrating yoke. By then, I would be working the controls like a wild man and stomping on the rudder pedals like I was mashing grapes into fine wine.

It usually didn't last much longer. When I finally reached the point of no return and we were about to go over on our back into a spin, he would grab the yoke, say quietly, "I've got it." and in an instant we would be back in straight and level flight. Then he would tell me what I had done wrong, show me what I had done, show me how to do it right with me following him through the controls, and give me the controls back. Then it was my turn again.

We did it over and over and I learned a lot. I would be so tired after an hour of this that I would literally fall out of the plane when we got back to the airport. At night I studied for my written, examined charts, and tried to unravel the mysteries of my new, circular slide-rule-type flight calculator. And I was having the time of my life!

* * *

Over the next two weeks, I took five lessons and we spent all that time doing turns, stalls,* accelerated stalls, approach stalls, departure stalls, steep turns, slips, and a lot of takeoffs and landings. On September 2, we did takeoffs and landings at Sherman Army Air Base at Leavenworth, Kansas for the whole lesson. I did great! Every takeoff was straight down the runway and every landing was a greaser. Virgil didn't have to touch the controls once, and I was thinking that I was the hottest smoldering boulder to ever touch a yoke. Virgil didn't look very pleased and I was wondering why. I didn't know what he was setting me up for until it was too late. I found out the next day.

On September 3 we went out for another day of takeoffs and landings at Virgil's 1800-foot grass strip. My flying was appalling. I couldn't have found the ground if I had fallen out of the plane. The takeoffs went from one side of the runway to the other, accompanied by full-travel stomps on the rudder pedals; the landings were bouncing squat-

---

* A stall occurs when a plane gets into an attitude where the air passing over the wing can no longer provide lift, and the plane... falls. Sounds scary? It isn't. Every time a plane is landed properly, it stalls a few inches above the ground and quits flying. When the plane stalls three feet above the ground, it's called an arrival. We practice stalls to recognize and recover from those that happen unexpectedly — usually because of careless flying.

and-leave-its that had the birds falling from the trees laughing. Finally, after the wheels had quit coming up past the windows from the bounces and we were actually rolling on the ground, I braked her to a stop by the hangar.

I shamefacedly looked over at Virgil and was surprised to see him smiling. I figured that he was just relieved to be on the ground and that he was smiling over his decision to tell me to find another instructor. "Stop but don't shut her off," he said. Then he opened his door and got out. He turned around and shouted over the muffled thunder of the idling engine. "Take her around yourself and see what it's like."

With the speed of a striking fer-de-lance I reached over and grabbed his shirt (and quite a bit of flesh, too) in a death grip. "WHAT ARE YOU TALKING ABOUT??!!" I SCREAMED. "GET YOUR BUTT RIGHT BACK IN THIS PLANE. I'M NOT READY TO SOLO!"

"Yes, you are."

"NO, I'M NOT! I FLEW LOUSY TODAY!"

"No, you didn't." His face was starting to get red.

"HOW ABOUT ALL THOSE LANDINGS I BOTCHED UP?"

"Yeah, how about them? You corrected every one of them and I never had to touch the controls. Yesterday, you never screwed up and I wasn't sure you could get out of trouble. Now you've shown me you can. You're ready. Now shut up, do it right and don't give me any more gray hairs. Remember, she's going to lift off a lot quicker without me in there with you." He slammed the door and stalked off to the hangar where he kept his Swift.

I sat there in an absolute panic. Then, just to pass the time, I taxied her down to the end of the runway and tried to think of ways to get out of this mess. I did three or four mag checks, tested the controls ten or twelve times, worked the carb heat until it almost fell apart, and opened and closed the door a few times to see if the latch worked. I noticed the carpet needing cleaning. I stalled as long as I could, but I knew I finally had to face the moment of truth.

I took a deep breath and eased the throttle open. The engine roared and we started to roll, my feet beating a tattoo on the rudder pedals, my breath coming in gulps, and sweat dripping off my chin. This wasn't turning out at all the way I had envisioned my solo flight in all those daring fantasies. Where were the crowds of excited spectators led by buxom, blond, long-legged cheerleaders?

The Tweety Bird surged forward, accompanied by the throaty bellow of the mighty C-85, and the tail came up a lot sooner than I expected. Doing my usual taildragger shuffle, I kept her on the runway and she lifted off as sweet as you please and settled on a nice climbout. As we roared by the hangar I saw Virgil peeking out of the open door to see how I was doing. Suddenly, I realized I WAS ALONE IN THE PLANE FOR THE FIRST TIME! My terror factor, which had already been at record highs, went up a few more notches.

The crosswind turn was sort of shaky, what with my dancing feet and trembling hands. The downwind turn was the same. I had a case of tunnel vision that took in only the forward windshield. I started talking to myself as if Virgil were still beside me and I was telling him what I was doing.

Suddenly, everything was calm and I started to enjoy myself. "OK, carb heat on, throttle back to 1500 rpm, trim to hands-off at 80 mph... turn base... look for the runway... there it is... turn final... watch the ball*... trim to 70 mph hands off... there's the runway... line her up in the middle... throttle back... back more... trim to 60 miles per hour... looking good... don't hurt the plane... keep her straight." The scrub trees at the end of the runway flashed by and I started the flare. I waited. The nose came up and the runway slowly disappeared from view behind the cowling.

It was probably the best landing I have ever made. (Or ever will make.) The tailwheel kissed the ground just a fraction of a second before I actually felt the mains brushing the tops of the grass. The rollout was straight and without my usual frantic stomps on the rudder to keep her out of the beans.

I brought her to a stop. We just sat there on the ground, me and my plane, communing with each other. Her engine was chuckling to me congratulating me on the good landing; a sweet partnership had been formed. I slowly taxied back to the hangar, savoring the moment. It would never happen again. It was the most memorable and savorable "first" in my life.

---

* An instrument in the plane's panel contains a ball that remains centered if the pilot keeps the controls properly coordinated. See "SKID" in the Glossary for more details.

My chest swelled up so big that my shirt buttons were popping like shrapnel around the cockpit and the grin on my face was so wide that my face hurt. WHAT A FEELING! I HAD SOLOED!! Virgil opened the door and got in with a smile on his face. He looked at me and knew he didn't have to say anything. I don't know how Virgil had realized that "this was the time," but he was right. Maybe it's because he has been teaching flying for so long. He let me enjoy the moment a few seconds longer before getting back to business.

"Now that we've got that hurdle out of the way, we can get on with the business of teaching you how to fly. Take us back to Noah's." I was determined to show him that I was already an accomplished pilot. As we slowly taxied down to the end of the runway, I gave him a nauseatingly detailed, second-by-second account of the whole three-minute flight. I'm sure he was glad to finally reach the end of the runway so we could take off and I would have to shut up and fly the airplane.

The takeoff was great. The five minute flight to Noah's was great.

The landing was a disaster. My approach was too high, too fast and off-center. The side-slip I set up was too shallow. I was going to have to make a go-around. RATS! I could see the usual crowd of rail birds by the office waiting to pass judgment on the landing.

Virgil barked, "I've got it." I planted my feet on the floor and sat on my hands. He cranked her over into a 45-degree slip to the left and I watched the ground come up in my window with a speed that had me grabbing the seat rails so tight I left my fingerprints in the steel tubes. Just as I was getting ready to scream, he kicked her straight, leveled her out, and touched down in a kiss, kiss, gentle, perfect three-pointer at a speed that had us stopped in about three hundred feet. Man, was I impressed! If he could do that with this scraggly looking plane, then I could, too. I was determined to try harder. Someday I am going to be as good a pilot as he is. (It hasn't happened yet.)

"You'll be doing that in a few weeks, too, as soon as you get more used to her," he said.

"Uh huh, yeah, sure" I said.

The rest of the lesson was taken up with getting my logbook signed and the words "first solo flight" entered. It was a moment that I have savored often in the many years since, and I can remember it as if it happened yesterday. I'm sitting here right now looking at its tattered pages and smiling at the memories they bring back. Virgil is a saint; he earned his halo teaching me to fly.

Nothing came close to the thrill of that first solo flight — not even the check ride when I got my private license, three months to the day from my first lesson.

The moment that lives on to this day is remembering the words, "Take her around yourself and see what it's like." Everyone should go through that at least once in his lifetime. I didn't know it at the time, but the solo flight meant just what Virgil had said, that I was ready to learn to fly. The next several weeks were filled with lessons on flight maneuvers and countless takeoff and landings until Virgil was satisfied enough at my progress to sign me off for solo flight within the pattern. At night, I studied for the private pilot written test and practiced navigation problems with my circular aircraft slide rule, one of the most diabolical and confusing inventions of man since the discovery of the Rosetta Stone. All these preparations were getting me ready for the next big hurdle, the dual cross country flight.

Cross-Country Adventures

"Cessna 77212, What Are Your Intentions?"

It all started out so innocently. Virgil just casually mentioned at the end of one of our lessons that he wanted me to plan a cross-country flight of at least one hundred fifty miles so we could get the dual cross-country* out of the way. Then I could make my solo cross-country flights. I hadn't felt I was ready for cross-country flying yet, but evidently Virgil did. Our lessons lately had been composed of turns across a road, turns along a road, turns around a point, hooded instrument work (God! What a bear!), stalls, accelerated stalls, approach stalls, departure stalls, and any other neat little tortures that struck his fancy when I was doing things too well and he wanted to bring me down a notch or two. Virgil is a master of the surprise.

A few lessons after I had soloed, Virgil signed me off for touch-and-goes at Noah's Ark. I still look back fondly on those calm afternoons out at the airport boring a rectangular hole in the sky. Takeoff... crosswind turn... down wind turn... base leg... final approach turn... flare... bounce... bounce... takeoff... crosswind... over and over. Sounds boring but it isn't.

There's something positively sensuous about a perfect touch-and-

---

* Dual flight consists of student and instructor. Cross-country flights involve a landing at one or more airports other than your point of departure.

go sequence. The "perfect" takeoff is made without stomping grapes on the rudder pedals to keep her straight and the ball miraculously stays in the center on the crosswind, downwind, base, and final turns. The throttle is closed at just the right moment after the turn from base to final is made, and you don't have to touch it again throughout the whole approach. The wheels gently kiss-kiss the runway at just the right moment and the rollout is straight without any taildragger shuffle. Pure ecstasy! Believe me, after a hard day at school trying to unravel the mysteries of percent to 13- and 14-year-old eighth grade math students, an hour of touch-and-goes is a lot more effective than a double martini. You can feel the stress flowing out of you like water from a hose.

It's never the same, either. You can make ten great "greaser" landings while no one is watching at the airport, but just as soon as one guy comes out of the hangar to watch you land, you will bounce higher than the hangar roof. The height of the bounce is usually directly proportional to the number of rail birds watching you land. It's always a challenge. I still love to spend an afternoon doing touch-and-goes and highly recommend it to anyone with a need to unwind.

Touch-and-goes were almost as much fun as a lesson with Virgil, but since I had soloed he had become a somewhat harder taskmaster. He was always surprising me (scaring the stuffing out of me is another way of putting it) as he thought up new and interesting ways of shocking me out of my complacency. I was never bored, because Virgil was always stretching my learning to the limits by introducing new and interesting challenges. If I was doing too well, he could always simulate an emergency.

Virgil gave me my graduation emergency at night when we were on a right downwind for a landing on runway 33 at Sherman Army Air Base. There was a high overcast and it was blacker than a Lab in an oil spill. Winds were light and variable and visibility was unlimited. I had already made several landings that night, and because Virgil was in an unusually vicious, sadistic, creative frenzy, I was already a little rattled.

On my first landing, I used the mike and keyed the field's radio-controlled runway lights on when we were on right downwind. I used the landing light on the Tweety Bird and the touchdown on the 5000-foot-long runway was a piece of cake.

Virgil told me to do a touch-and-go and head around again. As we

35

Just as soon as one guy comes out to watch you land,
you will bounce higher than the hangar roof.

were on final I reached down to turn on the landing light and felt a hairy hand resting over the switch.

"It just burned out," a smug voice murmured in my ear.

"YOU DIRTY ROTTEN SLIME!" I screamed out in the dark cockpit.

"Yup," came the cheery response. The bum was enjoying this!

Boy, that landing was a revelation! Those landing lights are nice things to have. My arrival sounded like a bad accident in the kitchen. We really splattered! Those Cessna 120 fuselages really boom when you drop them in from five feet. I wanted to stop and see if anything had fallen off the plane. Virgil said to go on for another circuit. The next two landings under the same conditions were a lot better.

Then, naturally, since I was doing so well, Virgil changed the rules. The runway lights usually stay on about 15 minutes and we were getting set up for another landing without a landing light when the runway lights went out. I was reaching for the mike to key them back on when the Tweety Bird's landing light suddenly came on and the usual hairy hand yanked the mike out of my hand.

"Your radio just burned out!"

"You sadist! You could give the Marquis de Sade lessons!"

"Quit complaining, I fixed your landing light, didn't I? Now shaddup and gimme a good landing!"

This touchdown was a lot easier than the ones without the Tweety Bird's landing light. After we did about two no-runway-light landings he asked me to choose which one was the easiest. It was no contest. Give me the aircraft landing light any time.

"Are we going to try one without both?" I hesitantly asked. I was hoping that I wasn't giving him any new and wonderful ideas, but — not to worry.

"Hey, we don't have a death wish, we just want you to get good at this. Let's do one more and this time, everything electrical on the plane is going to work." I should have known that sneak had an ace up his sleeve.

I was just turning from base to final and speaking into the mike, advising the traffic what I was doing, when the engine suddenly went to full idle. I reached for the throttle and found Virgil's claw on the throttle knob and knew the worst. "Dead engine?"

"Yup" was the laconic reply from the right seat. "If you do this right, we'll go back to Noah's and I'll sign you off for solo night flight." I could sense him smiling from the right seat. By Gum! I'll show him! This landing was going to be a greaser.

My steely blue eyes narrowed to slits, my sinewy, powerful hands grasped the yoke in a death grip and my thin, sensual lips curved into a scornful sneer. I was ready. Let him do his worst. This was going to be a flawless landing. Down we went, the engine muttering quietly. We turned final and started our swift, almost silent descent into the Stygian abyss. The only lights visible were the lights of Fort Leavenworth from the left and the twinkling parallel lines of runway lights beckoning seductively in the distance from beneath the nose.

I was really keyed up for this one, and for some strange and wonderful reason the landing went great. The approach was smooth and the flare was so gentle you didn't even know I was doing it. We couldn't even feel when the wheels touched the pavement; only the rumbling from the tailwheel told us we were on the ground. The rollout was straight, without my usual frantic jabs at the rudder pedals. We slowly coasted to a stop.

I glanced over to the right and, in the reflected glare of the runway lights, saw Virgil sitting there with his mouth gaping open in amazement. His eyebrows were perched up on top of his forehead. He pursed his lips and gave a long, low whistle as his head swiveled slowly around towards me. He looked at me with awe-filled eyes. I knew he was really impressed. Since I thought I was still ten feet in the air when the wheels touched, I was pretty impressed too. Hey, I thought, keep him guessing.

"Heh... heh... heh... it went just the way I planned it," I chortled.

Virgil snorted derisively, "Yeah, sure it did! Let's go back to Noah's Ark." I could tell he was worried, though. He didn't know if I was lying or not. I smiled smugly in the comforting darkness.

Noah's Ark is 3000 feet long and a narrow 20 feet wide. The differences between landing on a 200-foot wide runway and a narrow one were major and frightening. I got it done but would hate to have to do it on a dark and stormy night with a blustery crosswind. (I think I would just fly the extra ten minutes to Kansas City Municipal and crash there. At least I would have a bigger and more appreciative audience.)

But the night was calm and the landing went great. We put the plane away and Virgil signed me off for solo night flight within a 10-mile radius of Noah's. Then he casually dropped The Bomb.

"Now it's time to take your dual cross-country," he announced. I was directed to plan a flight to Omaha, Nebraska, and return.

I gulped. Everyone had told me horror stories about getting lost, and I was sure that once I was more than five minutes from Noah's Ark I would be in "Indian territory." During some of our lessons, when Virgil had been working on improving my miserable instrument flying skills, I couldn't find my way back to the airport when the lesson was over. Sometimes we were less than ten miles away. This was going to be a real challenge.

I went down to Kansas City Municipal Airport the next day and bought Kansas City and Omaha sectional charts. I spread them out on the fully extended dining room table and started to plan. All three of my cats were willing and enthusiastic helpers in this endeavor. They kept chasing the rulers and plotters around the table as I drew, measured, and cussed.

I drew the line from Noah's Ark to Eppley Field and started to put in checkpoints every five miles, compass headings, ETAs (estimated times of arrival), fuel usage estimates, variations, deviations, miles traveled, miles left to go, VOR (radio navigation) frequencies and radials for triangulations, tower frequencies, alternate airports for each checkpoint, and the names of FBOs* with the types of gas they sold. The chart was covered with notations and numbers, and I had two sheets of notes covering all the checkpoints and everything else needed for a trip to the moon and beyond.

I had a lesson a few days later and showed the charts and notes to Virgil with a proud flourish. His jaw dropped and I could see him struggling with his emotions as he perused the perfectly planned flight. He seemed to be having trouble controlling his mouth. He finally spoke.

"What are you doing, Lindbergh? Planning a flight to Paris?"

Suddenly I had a hunch that he wasn't exactly impressed with my exhaustive flight planning effort. I had thought it was a masterpiece.

"What's the matter with it?" I asked in a little voice.

"Well for starters, we're only going 175 miles. You've got enough

* FBO: a fixed base operator that provides services such as fuel, flight training, aircraft rentals, and maintenance.

checkpoints for a thousand mile trip. Take out three-fourths of the checkpoints and shorten the notes down to one line of stuff for each checkpoint. You've got so much junk on that chart you'd need a co-pilot to fly the plane just so you could read the chart. You're going to be busier than a mosquito at a nude beach if you try to keep all that garbage up to date. Junk it and start over."

I slunk home with my tail between my legs and started over. The original charts were tattered rags by that point so I went out and purchased two more. The final result was a straight-line course with checkpoints about every 15 or 20 miles and minimum notes to clutter up the flight plan. Virgil OK'd this one and the flight was set up for the following Saturday. I spent the rest of the week refining the flight plan and trying to figure out the flight calculator I had purchased. In the quiet of my home, with the manual open and plenty of time to think, the calculator was easy to operate. I could whip up crosswind corrections like a pro and eat popcorn at the same time.

Saturday dawned hot, humid, and clear, with visibility of 15 to 20 miles and light winds. Aside from the heat, it was a pretty day to fly.

I arrived early, burdened with charts, flight plans, pencils, pens, aircraft plotter, flight calculator, a copy of AOPA's airport guide, official pilot sunglasses, binoculars, airsick pills, and a stopwatch around my neck. I clanked and clattered like a knight in armor when I walked. A detailed preflight, followed by a thorough scrubbing of the windows, finished the preparations. She still looked awful, with her peeling paint and patched wings, but she was clean. I nervously waited and soon the intimidating roar of the Swift told me that Virgil was coming. He greased her into another of his classic wheel landings and taxied up to me. As he got out, I could see him looking me over and checking out all my equipment. He shook his head and sighed.

"Do you think you forgot anything?" he sarcastically inquired.

"Nope," came my confident reply.

"Are you ready to go?"

"Yep."

"Is she full of gas?"

"Yes."

"Oil?"

"Four quarts. And I have two spare quarts in the back."

"Did you do a thorough preflight?"

"Yes."

"Do it again." I did. Virgil just followed me around and watched what I did. I must have done it right because he didn't say anything. I finished the preflight.

"Did you file a flight plan?"

Strike one! I hung my head and muttered, "No, I forgot."

Virgil looked down, slowly shook his head, sighed again and said, "Don't worry about it. We'll do it in the air over the radio."

He looked at me thoughtfully as I nervously hopped from foot to foot. "Did you go to the bathroom?"

Strike two! Three minutes later I came back from the corn field and told him I was ready to go.

Virgil looked at me, looked at the sky, muttered something to himself about easier ways to make a buck and said, "Well, we can't put it off any longer. Let's go." We mounted up.

We took off and the first thing Virgil made me do was file my flight plan with the Kansas City FSS (Flight Service Station). By the time that chore was finished, I found that I was already lost. The flight wasn't ten minutes old and already going downhill. After a little S-turning around I finally found my second check point (God only knows where the first one went) and we thrashed our uncertain way into aviation history.

"Can you figure your ground speed for the distance we have traveled since takeoff?"

"Hey... no problem." I flourished the flight calculator at him and started to spin the dial.

I was to find out immediately that I didn't know squat about working that hideous tool while trying to hold a course, maintain altitude, find checkpoints and keep answering the stupid questions the sadist in the next seat kept firing at me.

The worst question I kept getting over and over was, "Where are we now?"

I'd reply, "Somewhere along this line," pointing vaguely to the course line on the chart where I hoped we were.

"Could you show me exactly where we are, along the line?" he would politely ask.

"I don't have the foggiest idea," I would humbly reply while searching futilely for something out the window that even remotely resembled anything on the chart. I could see the river but that didn't help much in finding the exact place that old you-know-who wanted.

I won't tell you how many lakes that I had chosen as checkpoints were dried up that year. I also won't bore you with the way all little towns look the same from 4500 feet. I'm not sure how we finally got there, but at long last the bustling metropolis of Omaha appeared on the horizon.

I contacted the controllers in the tower and finally, after about 10 minutes of blundering around and being harassed by such questions as "Cessna 77212, what are your intentions?" I got on a right downwind for one-seven, the active runway. I was number five to land.

We had to extend our downwind for the 727 that was ahead of us. Then Virgil told me to ask the tower if we could extend it even more to avoid wake turbulence. When we were finally told to turn final, I was almost catatonic with fear. I'd never flown in this much traffic before and I didn't like it. Virgil just nonchalantly sat there, rared back in his seat whistling through his teeth as he watched the disaster unfold. When I completed the turn from base leg to final approach, he finally spoke.

"Did you see where the 727 just touched down?" he asked.

"Yeah," I mumbled through tightly clenched teeth. "So what?"

"Stay above his flight path on final and touch down 500 feet past where his wheels touched the ground. There's no wake turbulence when there's no lift."

I filed that fact for future reference and concentrated on making a landing good enough so the plane would probably fly again. We turned off the active and ground control directed us to the FBO, where a guy was already waving his arms and beckoning me to come over and buy his gas.

The engine shuddered to a stop and we fell out of the plane. It had been a two-hour, 12-minute flight.

While they were filling up Tweety, I closed our flight plan at the FSS, filed a new one, and got a weather briefing. I looked with dazed uncomprehending eyes at the weather chart as the briefer blathered on in a foreign language to me about dew points, convective buildup, low pressure areas, isobars, winds aloft, thunderstorms in France, the typhoon in the Sea of Japan, and the heartbreak of psoriasis.

I finished filing the flight plan for the trip back home and found

Virgil. He greeted me with his customary inquisition. "Did you file a new flight plan?"

"Yes."

"Get a weather briefing?"

"Sure."

"Understand it?"

"Of course. Sure. Well, uh, Most of it."

"Oh, good grief. Just exactly how much did you understand?"

"Somewhere in it he said, 'VFR all the way.'"

Virgil gave a big sigh and shook his head muttering something that had the word "idiot" in it. He cleared his throat, "Check the oil?"

"Yes."

"Give her a good preflight?"

"You bet."

"Pay for the gas?"

"No." Strike three!

I sauntered into the FBO, asked for my fuel ticket, and casually whipped out the ten-dollar bill that Sharon had graciously given me that morning for the flight. It was an advance on my weekly flying allowance. These people were going to know they were in the presence of a high-rolling, big spender. But I was used to paying for my 80 octane gas at little airports and was not quite prepared for the sticker shock of 100 octane low-lead at a big-time airport. MasterCard took care of the rest of the bill. I walked out of there muttering about pirates and bushwackers.

We jumped into Tweety and I fired her up and called ground control for directions. They blabbered on about active runways, traffic to avoid, winds and barometer settings, and turned us loose to go to the active.

We taxied to the active run-up area and I did my mag and control check. Everything looked great so I called the tower and told them we were ready to go. They came back and told us to stand by for several planes lined up on final to land. I pulled the power back and we waited as the parade began.

We waited. All the planes landed. We waited. And waited.

Several planes taxied around us and took off. The last one had people in it laughing and pointing at us. I knew my plane looked scuzzy but I didn't think she deserved ridicule! I finally knew then that something was wrong. I finally bit the bullet and looked over at Virgil.

"O.K. What am I doing wrong?" I mumbled.

"Look at your ammeter, Dummy!" he snarled as he pointed at the offending instrument.

It was showing a big discharge. I'd better explain that I had a Narco Mark 5 radio: a big, heavy, old-fashioned tube-type radio that draws enough current to power a small town. With the engine throttled back, the output from my generator fell so low that the radio quit working. I shoved in the throttle and the ammeter needle jumped up to show a charge. The radio came on with a crackle of static.

"Cessna 77212, do you read Omaha Control... Cessna 77212, do you read Omaha Control?... Cessna 77212, do you read Omaha Control... Cessna 77212, do you read... "

"Yes," I meekly responded.

"Are you having difficulties, 77212?"

"No. No difficulties. I just didn't know what I was doing."

"Are you ready for takeoff, 77212?"

"Yes, and if you will let me go I promise to never, never, never come back here and bother you again."

"Cessna 77212, you are cleared for an immediate takeoff. South departure approved. G'day."

Cross Country... Alone!

"You're a student pilot, aren't ya?"

After Virgil and I had returned from our dual cross-country to Omaha, he signed me off for my first *solo* cross-country flight. A short one. He still didn't trust me too far from home.

This first flight was a paltry little hop up the river to Mound City, Missouri. This brief jaunt was easy. Of course, when I got back I told Virgil that I flew a compass course correct to plus or minus two degrees, maintained a proper cruising altitude correct to plus or minus 20 feet, figured out mid-course wind drift corrections, compensated for compass deviation and variation and all the other little things that I knew he wanted to hear. I actually flew up the twisting and turning Missouri river at 500 feet AGL (above ground level — or in this case, above water level). It was a breeze. He signed me off for a longer second flight.

The second one was from Noah's Ark to Warrensburg, Missouri. This was easy, too. I did everything I had done on the flight to Mound City; the only difference was I substituted Highway 50 for the river. I didn't get lost on this one, either. This was fun! Who said this cross-country stuff was hard?

After those two short flights, I was bragging to Virgil about how good a pilot I was getting to be and this navigation stuff was no sweat. He smiled at me and told me to plan a triangular course with each leg of the triangle at least 100 miles and I had to stay in Missouri. I also had to make three landings at airports with operating control towers.

I gulped when he said that. I have a real knack of making an ass out of myself over the radio. That night I got out the sectional and started to measure and plan. Hmmmmmm. This wasn't going to be easy. I could take Interstate 70 east to Columbia, Missouri for 100 miles for the first leg but the second to Springfield was going to be harder.

Wait a minute. There are several huge lakes between Columbia and Springfield. Also, if you get really, seriously lost, there are four-lane highways you would eventually cross going in any direction. Only an absolute idiot could get lost going between those two points. This course was tailor-made for me. I stuck in a landing at Jefferson City to get the required three tower-controlled landings that Virgil wanted.

I drew on that sectional for a week. When I finished, there was a pretty triangular course laid out in red marker with true courses, magnetic courses, checkpoints, VOR triangulations, control tower frequencies, alternate airport control tower frequencies, and mileage numbers written beside the course line. It was beautiful and a pleasure to see. When I had my next flying lesson with Virgil, I unfolded the chart, flight plan forms, and detailed notes on the stabilizer of Tweety and showed it to him with a proud flourish. "Virgil, I'm ready for The Big One."

When Virgil looked at the chart, his eyebrows went up higher than I had ever seen them go before. As he carefully looked over the notes he noticed that the course to Columbia went parallel with I-70. He also noticed that the trip from Springfield followed Highway 71 north. His lips twitched and he had a sudden coughing fit.

"Is something wrong with it?" I anxiously asked.

"Why, no." he responded. "Not at all. This is a very well-thought-out flight plan. It's exactly what I expected to get out of you." His lips twitched again.

"I'm glad you like it." I said. "I planned this flight very carefully."

He had another coughing fit. "I'm sure you did. When are you planning to go on this odyssey?"

"This Saturday." I said. "Will you sign me off?"

He carefully wrote in my logbook that I had satisfied him that my flight plans were adequate for the flight and I was set.

* * *

Saturday finally arrived and the weather was great! Light northerly winds, and visibility was at least 20 miles. I got down to Noah's early in the morning. The Tweety Bird got a nit-picky preflight and three quarts of oil were stashed in the baggage area. The chart was carefully folded for the first leg to Columbia. I took two airsickness pills and laid airsick bags out in the passenger seat. Flight plan forms were clipped to the clipboard in the order that I would need them. After a final tinkle in the corn field, I was ready, as John Paul Jones so eloquently said, "To go in harm's way."

Tweety and I took off, the mighty C-85-12F roaring with anger and defiance. I had phoned in a flight plan to the Kansas City Flight Service Station when I rolled out of bed, so all I had to do was activate as soon as I was able to get them on the radio. The flight to Columbia was a joy. I kept I-70 about three miles off my left side and when I got to the Missouri river west of Columbia, I followed it, keeping it three miles away on my right side to Columbia Regional Airport. Flight time, one hour and 45 minutes, engine on to engine off. I enjoyed it.

I refueled Tweety and took off on our next leg to Jefferson City. That only took thirty minutes. Since I was going the rest of the way to Springfield non-stop, I decided to change tanks. I'd never done that in the air before and was afraid to do it. If that engine died, I would have followed it five seconds later. Anyway, as I landed at Jeff City, the tower asked me which FBO I wanted to go to. I told them neither one, I had just landed to switch tanks. There was a long silence on the radio.

Then the controller finally said, gently, "You're a student pilot, aren't ya?"

"How did you know?" I asked wonderingly.

"No special reason," he said. "You're cleared for immediate takeoff. Have a good trip."

The flight to Springfield should have taken only about one hour. It seemed like two years. Two hours and fifteen minutes later we landed. Talk about being lost! I had toured most of central Missouri. I had looked down at scenery not seen by humans since Indians stealthily stalked through the woods. Deserted railroad lines and small towns were avidly observed from 500 feet AGL while I was searching for recognizable landmarks.

I climbed up to 4500 feet and from there was able to see for miles in any direction. I finally found the Lake of the Ozarks, and from then

Talk about being lost! I had toured most of Central Missouri.

on, it was easy. Springfield came into view, I contacted the tower, and we landed. It was the first of many times that I wanted to kiss the ground when I got out of the plane. (But not the last. I've had a lot of dirt on my lips the past few years.)

The flight back to Kansas City was the longest leg. It took two hours and 15 minutes and I didn't get lost. All I had to do was fly the Highway 71 concrete compass and we miraculously arrived on time. I had my big trip cross-country requirements out of the way and was almost ready to take my private pilot check ride. Now, years later, I can say that the cross-country flights, solo, were the hump part of pilot training. Being lost far away from my home airport, and then finding myself, was the Rite of Passage for me.

I don't think a student pilot can ever feel as alone and abandoned to merciless fate as he feels on his first solo cross-country trip... when he finally, inevitably gets LOST! I know of some student pilots who abandoned pilot training after they landed from their terrifying first solo cross-country.

Hell! If you're afraid of getting lost, don't fly. Drive. Then you can stop at every little semi-deserted gas station and ask for directions. As far as I am concerned, knowing where you are takes all the fun out of it. Flying cross country, without using electronic marvels to navigate, takes a firm jaw... nerves of stainless steel... narrow, slitted eyes... lightning-fast reflexes... and a tendency to laugh at Danger. It's macho, seat-of-the-pants, hairy-chested flying at its absolute best.

Times have sure changed. Now, some student pilots use fancy radios such as loran and the Global Positioning System of satellite navigation. They simply dial in a destination while taxiing out to the runway, take off, follow some needles and land without ever having to look at a chart. I'm not sure all this technology is good for a student pilot, either. He might decide to depend on all these little magic boxes and really get burned. Capacitors quit capacitating, diodes quit dioding, alternators stop alternating, and a plethora of other things can go wrong to make you suddenly wish you had been following the chart and paying attention to where you were. If all your super-expensive little black boxes suddenly decide to throw craps on you, you'd better be ready to go back to good old-fashioned pilotage to navigate. Keep those charts out and follow where you are on them as you churn your merry way cross-country.

And make sure your charts are current. A friend of mine who is an air traffic controller at Kansas City International Airport once had a guy call in using a frequency that had been dropped three years before. When he finally landed, they made him come up to the tower where they chewed on him like hungry beavers on a sapling. If you are going to go cross-country and fly into busy airports, you'd better be prepared to play ball with the FAA or pay the price.

Stalls and Spins

They're fun when you do them right.

Virgil and I had just finished my usual Friday flying lesson. He had been unsuccessfully trying to cram some instrument flying knowledge into my poor little overstuffed brain and I was pooped. I think he was, too. Teaching the terminally dumb can be tiring.

As Virgil was filling out my logbook, he had muttered to me, "Do you think you can take three lessons this coming week?"

"Sure," I said. Then I started to think. "Why?" I cautiously asked. For some reason I sensed danger and tensed up inside.

"Well, you've got the hours. You've finished your cross-countries. We've done night flying, hooded instrument work, emergencies, and you've passed your written. Soooo... I've got you set up for your Private Pilot's check ride next Saturday up at Rosecrans Field. I want to give you some last minute fine tuning before you fly up there."

"CHECK RIDE?!?! I'M NOT READY TO TAKE A CHECK RIDE! WHY ARE YOU ALWAYS DOING THIS TO ME?" I wailed, looking at him in stunned disbelief.

I slumped against the cool, smooth side of the Tweety Bird in horrified shock. He loves to spring these little surprises on me. I think he knew how I would fuss and worry about whatever was coming up and decided to tell me at the last moment so my worry time would be less. Either that or he was an even bigger sadist than I thought.

Anyway, I tried to talk him out of it but, as usual, I lost. I was committed. We scheduled lessons for Monday, Wednesday and Friday. The check ride, I was informed, was set for ten o'clock Saturday morning. I started to worry in earnest.

I had found out through the grapevine that Virgil uses an FAA designated check pilot that he knows. This guy flies a Swift just like Virgil's and is known to be a pretty sharp pilot. He's also known to be pretty tough on the checkee in the left seat. Boy, a whole week to worry. I wasn't going to waste any time. I asked Virgil if he could squeeze me in for a lesson the next day. He said yes. I wanted to get some extra time in and sharpen up some skills.

The next morning I was out there early, doing my usual touch and goes for about an hour to get the old juices flowing. Then I flew about 20 miles west to get out from under the Kansas City TCA to practice some stalls and other assorted goodies.

I started with turns around a point, turns along a road, turns across a road and two-minute (standard rate) turns. Then I went on to more difficult (and fun) maneuvers that Virgil had signed me off to practice and perfect. I did some approach stalls, departure stalls, and accelerated stalls. They all went great except for the accelerated stalls. I never could get a good, dramatic break. By then, it was time for my lesson, so I floundered my way back to Noah's.

I entered the right downwind for one-five just as Virgil's gleaming silver Swift greased itself into a landing. Virgil got out, and I could see him standing with his hands on his hips as he watched my approach. I came in a little hot (too fast) and subsequently couldn't get her down as nicely as I wanted. As I bounced by the turnoff I could see Virgil waving. His mouth was opening and closing, too. I'm glad I couldn't hear what he was yelling.

As I got out of the Tweety Bird, he remarked with a grin, "I counted six landings. Are you going to log all of them?" I ignored him. As our lessons had progressed, he had become more and more the comedian. He had also become increasingly difficult to please. He still didn't cuss me out or thump me on the head, but he had quit giving the heartfelt sighs and shaking of the head that I was used to and was more disposed to make sarcastic remarks about my pathetic efforts.

Now, my lessons were kind of like a movie about Marine Corps boot camp. It is funny looking at it on the screen, but it would scare the living wits out of you if it was you facing that hairy screaming beast known as the D.I. But I still loved it. Even when I was doing rotten, I was having a great time and I knew that I had been lucky in having snared Virgil as my flight instructor. (Even though he fervently regretted it.) He loves flying, you see, and takes great pride in it, too. You can tell that he wants to pass that love on to anyone taking lessons from him. His striving for perfection is infectious, and even when I was alone I tried to emulate his treatment of a plane. Some pilots I have flown with rape a plane in the air, jerking the controls, stomping the rudder pedals and generally throwing the plane all around the sky. Virgil makes love to a plane when he flies. He's one smooooooooth stick and rudder man. Everything he does is planned and perfect.

I told him I was ready to go and he smiled, reached into the Swift, and brought out The Hood. His smile broadened and a devilish twinkle appeared in his eyes.

"Oh migawd!" I thought to myself. "He's going to put me through the grinder today!" While hooded instrument work was a lot of fun and one hell of a challenge, I STANK! Inwardly, I started to cry.

He smiled like a hungry timber wolf and barked, "OK, Hot Dog, let's go!"

We headed for our practice area just northwest of Tonganoxie, Kansas. As we were thrashing our way west under the Kansas City TCA, I asked him if we could try some accelerated stalls. He said sure. First, we did our 90 degree left and right clearing turns to see if anybody was flying beneath us. I slowed Tweety up to 55 mph, banked her over to the right 45 degrees, and hauled the yoke back into my belly. She thrashed around, shuddered and generally complained but finally mushed down and sank. I released back pressure and we were flying again in an instant. I never did get a good clean break. That was the problem I was having before Virgil showed up. I told him about it and he told me to sit on my hands and take my feet off the rudder pedals. I did.

He slowed her down to 55 mph, level flight. Then he banked her over 45 degrees to the right and really hauled the yoke back hard. My cheeks sagged in the G-force and we headed up in a 45-degree banked hard climb. She broke, and I mean she broke *quickly*! The left wing dropped and only the application of hard right rudder combined with the easing of the yoke kept us from dropping over into a spin. When I got my breath back, I was directed to do it several times to the left and right, and it wasn't until I finally began really hauling the yoke back like Virgil did that I started getting the good clean break. Every time we did something in the Tweety Bird that was considered a deviation from normal flight I fell more and more in love with the girl. You really had to abuse her to get her to bite you. If I was just nice to her, she would be nice to me. I just had to make sure that I never put her into a situation where I would have to get rough with her. Virgil was always saying to me, "Stay ahead of the plane, not behind it. You fly it, don't let it fly you." It was good advice.

* * *

After we had finished the accelerated stalls I casually asked Virgil how the classic stall-spin approach-to-landing accident happened.* He told me to climb to 3000 feet and set up for a landing. Then he told me to make a sharp turn as if I were going from base to final in a right-hand pattern, but to cross the controls to keep the wings level, and kick in a lot of right rudder to tighten the turn. Next, I was to increase back pressure as if I were trying to avoid the ground.

We were slowed to approach speed (60 MPH) and in the middle of the turn when it happened. The ball was glued to the left side of the skid/slip indicator and the plane sure didn't feel right. Suddenly, the right wing on the inside of the turn just quit, but the left wing on the outside of the turn was still flying. That plane snapped over to the right so quickly that my head banged against the window. That didn't bother me as much as the swirling kaleidoscope that greeted my bugged-out eyes through the windshield. The green and brown fields blurred into an enormous supreme pizza in front of me. We were in a spin! You know, spins really look very slow from the ground, but inside the plane, you feel like you are in a blender. I wanted out! Spins were supposed to be killers! I didn't like this at all. At every air show I had been to there had always been one performer who did "The Death Spin." I sure as hell didn't want to do a spin! Now, I was in one.

I screamed out, "AAAUUUGGGHHH!!! TAKE HER!" as we went over on our back and Virgil took over. He neutralized the controls, kicked hard left rudder and the spin was over in one turn. It took

---

* A spin is a stall that has gone rotational; it usually happens when one wing stalls before the other one.

about 400 feet to recover. If we had been at final approach altitude the results would have been a lot different. It would have bruised my plane! With all the extra altitude as a buffer, it was just a very effective and unforgettable demonstration. Once was enough! Getting the stuffing scared out of you is always the most effective way of making sure you don't forget something: Keep the ball centered when you are in a turn and don't make high-banked, sharp turns from base to final at low speed and low altitude! I saw a guy kill himself at Oshkosh two years later doing just that.

I was still a little shaken after that was over. Virgil looked over at me, saw the pale face and trembling hands and sighed. "Well, now's as good a time as any to do this... I've got her. Stay on the controls with me and feel what I do." I noticed a dangerous gleam in his eye. Inwardly, I cringed. I'd seen that look before.

He climbed her back up to 3000 feet and leveled off. Then he reduced power to 1900 rpm and hauled the yoke back. The airspeed started to bleed off, and Tweety began her pre-stall shuddering and complaining.

"What's the big deal?" I thought, "He's doing a partial power-on stall."

As she broke, I felt the left rudder pedal under my foot go all the way forward. She rotated over to the left and we rolled into a spin. Just as I was getting ready to open the door and vacate the premises, Virgil barked, "Look at the airspeed!"

I couldn't believe it! Here I thought we were going down at warp factor five speed and the ASI was indicating only 60 mph. We made a two-turn spin and Virgil kicked hard right rudder, released back pressure and we recovered in an instant.

"That, my boy," he remarked with a grin, "is a spin. There is nothing to be afraid of. A spin is only a rotating, descending stall." He went on, "If you remember to pull the power off and keep the yoke all the way back against the stops, initiating a spin is no big deal. Now, you're going to learn to spin today and before I'm through with you, you're going to be able to spin to the right and left and recover on your original compass heading."

"Uh huh, yeah, sure," I muttered. Suddenly it seemed that instrument training was a lot of fun. "I'd rather go under the hood and do some unusual attitudes, if you don't mind."

"Shaddup and do what I tell you," I was told.

We headed back up to 3000 feet and it was my turn. You know, in a gentle little lady like a 120 or 140, a spin takes a little planning. If you don't have some prop blast going over the rudder when she breaks, all you get is a mushy spiral. If you don't keep the yoke all the way back against the stops, you get a spiral dive (which is not good). If you want to spin to the right, against the torque generated by the prop, you have to really have a lot of prop blast over the rudder to get her to twist over. It took many tries, but I was soon just a-twistin and a-turnin in the skies like a wild man. This was really fun! Recovering on the same heading took about a 20-to 30-degree anticipation factor. When I had done several one-turn spins in each direction to Virgil's satisfaction, he set me up for the final exam. I lined up on a road and started my entry. Keeping in 1900 rpm, I eased the yoke back and waited for the complaining to start. Just as I felt her sigh and give up, I kicked full left rudder. As she started her rotation, I yanked the yoke back against the stops and pulled the power all the way off. We rolled over and started to spin. Now that I had done several spins, it seemed really slow. I saw the road appear on the left side of the windshield and stomped full right rudder, releasing back pressure at the same time. We stopped rotating, and were suddenly back to level flight on the same course as before. Altitude lost: 400 feet.

Virgil had been sitting beside me with his arm on the seat back whistling nonchalantly as we went through the whole maneuver. Another aviation bugaboo had been destroyed. Spins are fun! You just have to know that like anything else in aviation, you must respect them. Learn them in the company of a flight instructor and do them only in a plane that is certified for spins. They have to be done right or you could still get bitten. Cross-control induced spins are another matter. I still don't like to do them because they hit sooooo quickly.

That ended that lesson. Virgil told me we would do the instrument final on our next lesson. We snaked our way back to Noah's and I did another one of my kangaroo wheel landings. It only took about four bounces before I was finally able to nail her down. As we went yo-yoing down the runway, Virgil just sat there with his head bobbing like one of those statues in the back window of a '57 Chevy. "You really need (KASPRONG!) to work (CLATTER) on these (BOUNCE) a lot before (BOOM-CLATTER) next Saturday," he quietly observed as we went bounding down the runway.

* * *

The next day was a no-lesson day, so I went out to practice what I had been taught the day before. Tweety and I went out west to Mc-Louth, Kansas, totally out of the Kansas City TCA, and climbed up to 5000 feet. I started off with approach stalls, worked my way up to departure stalls and finished off with some accelerated stalls. All went well. Then I tried a few spins. The first thing I noticed was that the plane was a lot harder to spin with just one person in it. The lighter weight must have been the cause. Anyway, I finally got her to twist over to the left and the recovery was also easier with the lighter weight. I did several to the left and then tried a two-turn spin. I took a little longer to recover because she did seem to wind up a little tighter doing two turns, but kicking full opposite rudder and releasing back pressure gave a quick, positive end to the spin.

Then I tried a few spins to the right. These were a lot harder. The first few I tried were failures. I couldn't get a good clean break and they ended up as mushy spirals to the right. The next time, I added more power and had a pretty good up-angle on her when the break I was looking for finally happened. We were pointing up at about 60 degrees when she finally broke. She snapped over on her back and after two turns I kicked full left rudder and released back pressure on the yoke. The rotation quickly stopped and I pushed forward on the yoke to complete the stall recovery.

My heart almost stopped! Something had jammed the controls!! The yoke wouldn't go forward any further than half-way!!! Tweety was mushing along tail low and shuddering on the ragged edge of a stall. I kept trying to push the wheel forward but it wouldn't go. Whatever was holding it felt kind of spongy-firm but I sure didn't want to push too hard and break something critical. I found that by adding power and pushing forward on the wheel I could maintain level flight at 50 mph.

I started to mess with the trim wheel and found a little relief to the problem. If I trimmed the trim tab for full up elevator and kept pushing hard on the yoke, I could get a slight descent and maintain control at 60 mph. This was because the tab became a very small elevator attached to what was now a non-moving extension of the stabilizer. A trim tab moves in the opposite direction of the desired direction of travel you want the control surface to move.

What that boiled down to was that I had discovered a way to keep from tearing up Tweety. The flight back to Noah's was the longest 15 minutes of my life. My arms were shaking from having to keep the forward pressure on the wheel and my heart was pounding from fear and panic.

I floundered into the pattern at Noah's, and by easing the throttle back was able to line up on the runway and mush my way down to the threshold. By cutting power, I settled Tweety into a rather bouncy three-point landing. I taxied over to the hangar and cut the switch. Throwing my seat belt off, I practiced deep breathing for a time and finally got out of the plane.

I went over to the shade of the hangar and sat, letting the cool breeze dry the sweat on my fevered brow. It took a while.

After I had recovered, I grabbed a flashlight and crawled under the instrument panel and looked around. One of the antenna leads had a big loop in it and had hooked over one of the arms of the control yoke under negative Gs. I could have just pushed a little harder on the yoke and unplugged the antenna from the radio and had no problem. Since I didn't know the cause of the problem at the time, I hadn't wanted to take the chance. It took about ten seconds to unhook the loop from the control arm.

I put Tweety away, drove up to the hardware store, bought an armful of nylon wire ties and headed back to the airport. Then I spent a steamy hour cussing behind the panel tying up every loose object I could see.

From then on, once a month I would stick my head under the panel and see if anything was hanging free. I often wonder, when I am flying with another pilot in a "strange" plane, what it looks like under his panel. If you have never looked under one, try it and see what you see.

And if you are a pilot and have never had training in spins, find an instructor and try them out. It won't take very long to destroy a bugaboo.

The Instrument Lesson

Or... Terror Under the Hood!

This lesson was going to be my instrument final from Virgil. Once again, I went out early and did some touch and goes to loosen up before my mentor arrived. When I taxied up to the hangar at his field, he was waiting with the hood in his hand and a smile on his face.

"Are you ready?" he asked.

"Yep," I responded. "No prisoners today."

"How long were you up before coming here?" he queried.

I told him I had flown about thirty minutes. He smiled and said that should have wound up the gyros enough. I didn't know what he meant. That old feeling started to race up and down my spine.

"Taxi down to the end of the runway and get her centered and pointed straight down the runway."

I did what he said, while wondering what new torture he had planned for me today. When we got down to the end of the runway, I got Tweety aimed right down the middle.

Virgil turned to me and started to put the hood on my head.

"What are you doing?" I cried, as I ducked and dodged trying to avoid that hideous instrument of torture.

"You're going to make an instrument takeoff," he said with a smile.

"You can kiss my rosy red dimpled cheeks, too," I told him.

As usual, protesting did no good. The hood was jammed down over my ears and all I could see was the sparse instrument panel in front of me. Vertigo immediately set in and we were sitting still!

"Set your directional gyro at 360 degrees and keep it there during the takeoff roll," he yelled in my ear. "When you get 60 mph, rotate, maintain a 360-degree heading and keep your airspeed at 65 to 70 until we get 800 feet above ground. Then you can adjust your directional gyro to what your magnetic compass indicates."

I knew it wouldn't help to beg or stall for time, so I locked my eyes on the directional gyro, artificial horizon, and airspeed indicator while I slowly eased the throttle forward. The mighty C-85-12F bellowed with joy and we began to rocket and bounce down the runway. I really had to concentrate hard but we got through 40, 50, 55, and 60 mph while keeping the DG needle centered on the "0" (360 degrees). When she indicated 60 mph I eased the yoke back and could tell by the altimeter needle's slow clockwise rotation that we were going up. When we got 800 feet above the ground I set the DG to the compass reading.

Following Virgil's commands, I did turns, climbs, descents, and two-minute turns as he barked out orders, comments, suggestions and, when I didn't listen to his suggestions, sarcastic remarks about stupidity and bull-headedness.

Then came the part I was dreading, Unusual Attitudes.* To teach me to make a safe recovery, Virgil would take the controls and, with me still under the hood and looking down at my tummy, he'd horse the plane into something like a 45-degree bank with the airspeed pushing either the lower or higher limits. My job was to get her back to straight and level, as quickly and smoothly as possible, by looking at the instruments and figuring out what had "gone wrong." I wasn't good at this but I sure did have fun trying to get good. I had been studying, though, and was going to try a new strategy. I was going to do what Virgil said: depend on the instruments and ignore what my ears told me.

"Fold your arms on your chest, put your feet on the floor and look down at your belly button," I was told.

I did.

All I could see was the sweat dappled, bulging-at-the-seams belly of my Lounge Lizard T-shirt. I could tell from the way my body was

---

* An unusual attitude is a condition a plane can get in if, for instance, a pilot bumbles into a cloud, loses his ground reference, and becomes disoriented.

straining against the seat belt and the way I was getting thrown around the cockpit that Virgil was doing strange and wonderful things to Tweety. According to my inner ear, we were upside down.

Suddenly he barked, "OK, you've got it."

Virgil had taught me to use what I like to call a sequential-simultaneous procedure in unusual attitude work. The first thing I was taught to look at was the airspeed indicator: it was indicating 120 mph. That's fast for a Cessna 120 (it's the bottom of the yellow arc on the dial). I pulled the power off. At the same time the power was coming off, I looked at the artificial horizon. We were in a nose-down spiral dive to the right. I leveled the wings and eased back on the yoke. Once everything was stable, I climbed back up to the altitude and course we were on before he did it to me. I might add that all of this was done in one continuous, coordinated, smooth, flowing, sensuous, catlike movement of the controls. (Totally unlike my usual jerky, foot-stomping, yawing from side-to-side, eyeball-bugging, convulsive seizure on the controls Virgil was used to.)

I peeked over from under the hood at Virgil. He was sitting there in stunned silence. He pursed his lips and gave a long, low whistle as his head swiveled slowly around to me. He looked at me with awe-filled eyes. I had done good!!! I'd never done it right before. I was finally on the scoreboard. Virgil: 467, me: 1.

"That wasn't so hard," I smugly said with a tolerant smile. Looking back on the episode now I know that bragging like that was a grievous error. It was like hurling gas onto an open fire.

Virgil's eyes narrowed and his lips curled into a sneer. "Oh Yeah?... OK, Hot Stuff. Put your head back down."

Rats! I wished I hadn't said that. For at least a minute I was thrown all around and up and down in the cockpit. This time I was sure that Tweety was on her back a few times before I was told to take over. Finally, it was my turn. "You got it, Ace!" he barked.

Airspeed: 50 mph and decaying. Throttle in. The artificial horizon showed a steep climb with a 45 degree bank to the left. I turned the yoke to the right and shoved forward. Five seconds later we were back to straight and level flight.

"Yo Momma!" I crowed. "This is easy. Can't you give me something hard?" (Fools rush in.)

Virgil's face got red and I could see he was hatching some new and obnoxious plan as I beamed proudly at him. Suddenly he smiled sweetly and softly said, "OK, Smartmouth, now it's my turn. Assume the position." I immediately regretted my lofty attitude and started to whimper, whine, and plead for mercy. It was too late. My pleas fell on deaf ears.

"Look at your belly, Fatso," he snarled.

Boy, this was strange! Nothing seemed to be happening. We weren't thrashing around any. Then he told me to look up. My blood chilled and my toes curled in my stylish K-Mart $9 blue-light-special tennis shoes.

That rotten bum! He had caged (locked in position) the artificial horizon and directional gyro. He had also covered the airspeed indicator with a piece of paper. I was flying on the compass, altimeter, needle and ball and rate-of-climb. PARTIAL PANEL! This was not good. The last time I had tried this the results were really stinky. I tried to peek out from under the hood and got a nasty shot in the ribs from his elbow. "Keep your head down, dummy" he snarled in my ear.

For about a minute everything was fine. Straight and level wasn't too hard. Then he told me to make a ninety degree turn to the left and lose 200 feet of altitude. I gently banked to the left and tried to keep the needle under the dog house on the turn indicator. The magnetic compass started to spin like a phonograph record and after about 30 seconds something didn't feel quite right. The ball was centered but the needle kept showing an increasing rate of turn to the left. The rate of climb was showing an increasing loss of altitude and the altimeter was going nuts. The engine was gaining in rpm. Virgil finally quietly said, "OK, look up!"

Raising my head, I could see I was in a graveyard spiral to the left. I straightened her up and looked over at Virgil. Now it was time to get serious. "What'd I do wrong?"

"As soon as you saw that needle showing excessive rate of turn you should have applied opposite rudder and aileron until the needle showed no turn and the rate of climb stabilized and went back to zero. If the needle and ball are both centered, you're going straight. Maintain altitude and course until the compass settles down and try again. Keep these partial panel turns very shallow and gentle. I hope you never get into a mess and have to do this for real. It's not fun for anyone. Now, go back under the hood. We're going to do this some more."

After about ten more endless minutes of turns, climbs, and descents under partial panel conditions, he seemed pleased. I was told to look back down at my tummy again.

Again, nothing happened but when I was told to look up everything was back to normal. I breathed a big sigh of relief and looked at Virgil. We were 1500 feet AGL directly above the airport. Just then, with no warning, and a suddenness that made my heart stop, the engine dramatically quit. My hair stood up so quick it lifted the hat on my head. (My hair got a lot of exercise when I was learning to fly.)

I moaned under my breath, "Oh good grief!" I knew what had happened. He'd shut the fuel off on me *again*. At least this time I didn't get scared. This man loved to throw emergencies at me all the time. Night, day, takeoff, landing, he just had no sense of propriety. It was his favorite form of outdoor recreation. Was there no limit to his persecution of his poor students? Obviously not! I looked at Virgil. He blinked his eyes and smiled happily at me.

"Your engine just quit," he announced gleefully.

I knew better than to argue by this time.

Silently, we started down.

* * *

I do have to admit that I was getting a lot better at this emergency stuff. Three months back, the first time he shut the gas off on me, I went into a catatonic state of shock. I just sat there with my eyes bugged out like a spooked owl. My heart was pounding and my hands were clutching the yoke in a death grip. Well, at least my left hand was clutching the yoke — my right hand was flipping every switch on the instrument panel and pumping the throttle like Quasimodo trying to ring in the new year. Nothing worked. I finally looked over at Virgil and he was sitting there with a smug, happy smile on his face and his hand on the fuel tank selector lever — it was in the OFF position!

He then smiled gently at me and, in the eerie engine-less quiet, had softly asked, "Which way is the wind blowing?"

I looked at him in slack-jawed amazement. "DON'T YOU KNOW??!!"

"Sure," he answered. "But I want *you* to tell me."

I answered with my world-famous blank look that I reserve for the times the school principal asks for some teachers to volunteer for a committee.

Virgil smiled sweetly again. The wind was whistling shrilly by the windows as Tweety headed down. "Don't you think it would be a good idea if you picked a field out there for us to land on? I think that would be nice." The rat was actually enjoying this.

I still sat there in sweaty, frozen terror. Virgil finally realized that nothing was going to happen and talked me into a landing approach for a big, recently harvested wheat field. When he could see that I had the field made, he turned the gas back on. As the mighty C-85-12F returned to life he smiled at me again. "Interesting, wasn't it?"

With hurt eyes I looked accusingly at him. "You are not a nice man."

He looked at me sternly. "WHEN YOU ARE FLYING A SINGLE-ENGINE AIRCRAFT, ALWAYS, ALWAYS, ALWAYS, WHILE YOU ARE IN THE AIR, BE LOOKING FOR AN EMERGENCY FIELD IN CASE THE ENGINE FAILS. I am going to give you emergencies throughout our training and I want you to be ready in case the Big One ever does happen."

He did, too. Takeoff, landing, cruise, *night* (that was a Jim-Dandy!). I got them all.

When you are flying over a big city, sometimes there's nothing in sight that could even remotely be considered as an emergency landing site. That's when the disconcerting aeronautical phenomenon known as "Automatic Rough" can be encountered. It occurs just as soon as that last golf course has disappeared behind you and nothing can be seen in front of you but housing developments with winding roads and power lines. For no reason at all, the engine will start to sound "strange." A new vibration will start to stutter through the airframe. All the gauges are in the green but something is just not right.

You fly on, anxiously watching the ground and the instruments. The engine gets rougher. Your heart starts to pound and your palms sweat. The gauges still say that everything is copacetic. Then a four-lane highway or another golf course appears in front of you. The engine mysteriously smooths out. It never fails. It's during Automatic Rough situations that you wish you had paid more attention when your instructor was talking about emergency situations and what to do when things start to turn sour.

Now, whenever I am in the air I am constantly looking at the ground and gauging whether I think I could make a certain field from the altitude I have. I think Virgil did a good job.

✻ ✻ ✻

Anyway, back to my last emergency. "I want you to put her down on the runway," he said as we silently glided down. Mount Muncie International Airport's 1800-foot runway is surrounded by large, 100-acre fields in the Missouri River bottoms but this was going to be a little more challenging than his "usual" emergency. This time, he was telling me exactly where he wanted me to land—on the runway—with no engine. This man was nuts!!!

Virgil took a look out the right window and I furtively tried to turn the fuel back on. He countered that move by lifting up his foot and stomping on my hand. That sure ended that. Sucking on my mashed blue fingers, I whimpered and whined as I looked around, tears running down my cheeks. Virgil just sat there and glared at me.

"Now, like I said," he grated in his best John Wayne voice, "land her on the field."

We were now at about 700 feet AGL and I did a 360 to lose some altitude. We still seemed to be a little high so I started to do another 360. Halfway through the turn the engine suddenly came back on with a roar. I looked over at Virgil with raised eyebrows.

"How come you gave me the engine back?" I asked.

"You'll never make it." He pulled the carb heat on and retarded the throttle to 1200 rpm. "Go ahead. Try it."

I finished the 360 and lined up on the runway. He was right. We were going to be about 500 feet short of the runway. I added power so we would make the runway and prepared to land.

"Make it a touch and go and do it again," he said. "And this time, slip instead of trying to turn if you're less than 400 feet above the ground. You can figure on about 300 to 400 feet altitude loss in a power off 360 *if you are really good*. Slips are better. Practice this 'emergency' the next couple of times you go out."

The next landing went OK and I was told to show up Friday for my "crosswind landing" final—the last lesson before the check ride.

Friday came and I can still hear Virgil's voice screaming in my ears as the wheels finally squashed down on the runway, "FULL AILERON INTO THE WIND! FULL AILERON! FULL

AILERON!" Damn! How could something this much fun be so demanding?!

The last two landings were good enough to satisfy him and he told me to practice wheel landings for an hour after he left. I was told to be down at Noah's Ark airport at eight in the morning with all my assorted materials for the check ride. He would sign my logbook and clear me for the cross-country flight up to St. Joseph, Missouri, where I was to meet the check pilot.

The Check Ride

The moment of truth arrives.

I didn't sleep much that night. The forecast for the following day was sunny (good) and clear (good) with gusty southerly winds (*bad*). That meant it was going to be bumpy. I was also worried about crosswind landings in high, gusty winds. Wheel landings — I didn't even want to think about them.

I had spent every night that week studying sectional charts and working my flight computer. I still wasn't very adept at using all the functions of which it was capable and hoped I wasn't going to get too many in-flight questions that would require its operation. I did weight and balance and crosswind course problems until they were running out my ears. I went around the house in a daze muttering, "Can Ducks Make Vertical Turns... East is least and odd, West is best and even... Accelerate, North; Decelerate, South... gas is six pounds a gallon... " until I thought Sharon was going to kill me. I didn't think I was ready. Pre-test jitters got me as usual.

At 5:00 in the morning, the wind roaring in the trees outside our bedroom window woke me up. I reached over, picked up the phone and dialed Virgil's number. The phone rang about 10 times before he picked it up and grunted something into the mouthpiece. I'm still not quite sure what he said. It sounded foreign. Maybe he is an enemy agent.

"Virgil, this is Dick." I said. "Don't you think it's a little windy for a check ride today?"

He sputtered like a flooded engine for a few seconds and then screamed in the phone, "YOU HAVE YOUR BUTT DOWN AT THE AIRPORT AT EIGHT O'CLOCK!" Then he slammed the phone down. My ear rang for a full minute.

Well, I guess that settled that. He didn't have to get so huffy. I started to gather together all my equipment for the test.

I arrived at Noah's early. I did several preflights and settled down for a last minute studying of charts for the oral part of the test. Soon the roar of the Swift told me Virgil was coming and I watched as he landed and taxied up to where I was nervously standing.

"Are you ready to go?" he barked as he jumped out of the Swift.

"No!" I cried. "I'm scared and it's too windy." (Maybe he would take pity on me.)

(He didn't.) "Got your logbook?"

"Yes."

"Student pilot permit?"

"Yep."

"Medical certificate?"

"Yep."

"I've got a hood in the Swift for the instrument check."

"No need," I said. "I made my own." I picked it up with a flourish. I had taken an old baseball hat and by using duct tape and some cardboard from a six-pack of beer, made my own instrument hood. It looked like a cross between the flying nun's headgear and a run-over cat, but it worked.

Virgil looked at it, slowly shook his head, and sighed again from the bottom of his very soul. "There is no way that a student of mine will show up for a check ride using that. You'll take the one in the Swift." He threw mine in the trash. I was really hurt.

"Do you have your fee for the check ride?"

Uh Oh!... I'd forgotten to sneak some cash from Sharon's purse. "Does he take MasterCard?" I hopefully asked.

"Oh for gawd's sake!" he moaned. "What did you bring?"

Now I really felt bad. I just looked at the ground and whimpered.

"Here, you can pay me back later," Virgil said while digging in his wallet... "if you live." He thrust the money in my hand and signed off my logbook for the flight up.

I tried one more time to convince him that it was too windy to take a check ride but, as usual, I lost.

Virgil looked at me and said in a low, ominous voice, "If he ever has to take the controls from you, it's over and you've flunked. *I have never had one of my students flunk a check ride.* It makes me look like I didn't do a good job teaching them to fly. Good luck and goodbye."

Boy! Talk about pressure. As I taxied out to the active, I was praying that I wasn't going to be the first.

The flight to St. Joe took only about 15 minutes with the 25-knot tail wind at 2000 feet. The tower said the wind was from 190 degrees at 18 knots. The active runway was one-seven. As I was landing, I thought to myself, "This is a 20-degree crosswind at 18 knots. It should be enough to satisfy a check pilot." I started to hope.

I taxied up to the office, shut her down, got out, and went in. Inside there were three men standing at the counter drinking coffee. One rugged-looking individual glanced at me and said, "Dick Starks?"

"Yes," I quavered.

"I'm your check pilot. Give me your papers."

I gave him all my logs, certificates, and the money. He stuffed the money in his pocket, looked over everything else, and grunted. "I weigh 175 pounds. Figure out a weight and balance for me and you. Also, I want you to plot a course from here to Topeka. Here's the latest weather data." He threw a slip of paper on the table. "Get to work." He went back over to the counter and resumed his conversation with the guys.

I spread out all my stuff on the table. Sectional chart, plotter, flight calculator, Texas Instruments calculator, straight edge, AOPA airport book, pencils, FAA flight plan form, pens, highlighters, erasers, and scratch paper. He strolled over to see what I was doing.

His eyebrows lifted up as he looked at all my equipment. Then he nodded his head and remarked, "Oh yeah, Virgil told me about you."

I gulped. He went back to shooting the breeze with the other guys in the office, and I started to draw lines, erase, worry, and sweat. After about fifteen minutes he came over and said, "OK, let's have it."

I gave him my chart, flight plan notes and weight and balance results. He looked them over for about three or four minutes while I sat in silent anguish. I knew the oral part of the test was coming up.

He spread out the Kansas City sectional chart in front of me and pointed to the Napoleon VOR box where the VOR frequency was displayed. The lower right hand corner of the box had a little filled square on it.

"What's this little square mean?" he asked.

My stomach curled into a knot. "I don't know."

He looked silently at me for a few seconds. "OK," he said pointing to the Johnson County VOR box. "What does it mean when the VOR frequency is underlined?"

My toes knotted up in my shoes and sweat started to run down my forehead into my eyes. "I don't know that, either," I replied in a low, wretched voice. I wondered if he was going to flunk me now and make me call Sharon so she could drive me home. He just looked at me silently.

Just then the line boy tapped me on the shoulder. "Excuse me, sir, your plane is rolling down the ramp."

Sure enough, there she went, merrily rolling down the ramp with two guys in hot pursuit. The parking brake had let go and the gusty wind had taken over. I joined the cheering crowd chasing her as she wandered down the ramp. When we pushed her back to the tie-down area I tied the wings and chocked the wheels. Then I went to face the rack of the inquisition.

He was sitting there with a thoughtful look on his face as I came in. I sat down and the silence was broken only by his pencil tapping on the table. He finally shook his head and sighed (just like Virgil) and went back to studying my flight plan and weight and balance results.

He started to fire more questions at me about charts, FARs, engine operation, weather, radio terminology and everything else associated with flying. Thankfully, I was able to dredge up correct answers to them from then on. This lasted about 45 minutes. Finally he threw all the papers down. "OK on the oral. Let's go fly."

"How about those first two questions I couldn't answer?" I asked.

"Oh heck," he replied. "No one ever knows what those mean. I just keep hoping that some day someone will. Everything else you did was fine."

We went outside. When he first saw the Tweety Bird he stopped

"Excuse me, sir, your plane is rolling down the ramp."

short and stared. I've got to admit that at that time, before the rebuild, she wasn't a sight to inspire confidence or enthusiasm. The sunlight wasn't kind to her with her faded, peeling paint and patched, scabrous wings.

"Is *this* what you and Virgil have been flying?" he asked.

I nodded my head.

"Good Grief!" (I didn't think she looked *that* bad.)

"She's really a very good plane." I said.

"Has Virgil checked it over?" (Virgil's also an experienced A & P mechanic.)

I nodded my head again.

"OK, I guess," he doubtfully said. "Let me see you do a preflight."

I started off with the most nit-picky preflight that Tweety had ever gone through. He followed me around as I did it and then asked me if I was through. I nodded my head wondering what I had forgotten.

"OK," he said. "Get in."

We loaded up and strapped in. He looked over at me expectantly. I got out my checklist and started to check things off verbally.

"Oil level... Check. No water in gas... Check. Walk-around preflight... Check. Controls free... " I pressed full right and left rudder, rolled in full aileron both ways and checked for full elevator travel up and down. "Check. Fuel on fullest tank... Check. Brakes set... Check. Carb heat off... Check. Mixture full rich... Check. Trim Tab in takeoff position... Check. Master switch on... Check. Throttle cracked... Check. Prime two shots... Check. Clear Prop... " Even though the ramp was deserted, I opened the window and screamed, "CLEAR PROP" He jumped in his seat and glared at me. I reached up to turn on the mags. Uh Oh! No key.

"Heh, heh, heh. I left the keys in my pocket."

He just looked at me with no expression on his face.

I am a large guy. I call it Big Boned. Everybody else calls me Fatso. They don't know that my big bulky clothes conceal the body of a Greek god covered with muscles that ripple and coil like a pit full of enraged pythons. I wear loose-fitting garments so that crazed, love-starved women won't chase me down the street and make my life a living hell. Anyway, I couldn't get into my pants pocket in the close confines of the cockpit so I had to unstrap, get out of the plane, get out the keys, and then get back in. He just sat there looking at me and slowly shaking his head. I wondered if he was even going to let me start the engine. I put the key in the switch, turned the mags on, and gave him a sickly grin. "I'm ready now."

"Virgil was sure right about you," he growled, shaking his head. "OK, start her up."

I screamed out, "CLEAR!" again and started her up. As soon as I got oil pressure, I called the tower and we got all the numbers and were told to taxi to the active. It was still runway one-seven. The wind was still from 190 degrees at a steady 18 knots.

The first thing he wanted was a short field takeoff. That was easy with a 20-mph headwind. As soon as we lifted off he told me to ask the tower for a stop-and-go pattern. They said OK, so we started around. I turned final and he told me he wanted "a short field landing on the numbers."

I trimmed her for 60 mph hands-off and we started down. With that much headwind it was easy. We hit on the runways numbers and were stopped soon after. It had taken a little crab and side slip to make the landing, so I hoped that was all the crosswind work he wanted me to do. Wrong.

He told me to take off again. Just as I turned crosswind he told me to tell the tower we were going to do another stop and go but we wanted to use runway one-three for the next landing. That was a sixty-degree cross-wind from the right. My nightmare was coming true. It was time to try my number one evasion tactic... bamboozling.

I looked over at him and said, "Sir, that exceeds the crosswind component of this particular aircraft model."

He looked at me with a tolerant smile. "No it doesn't. I've owned a few 120s. It can handle several more knots than this with no problem."

Rats! Oh well, at least I tried. Virgil must have told him a lot about me. This was not going to be fun! When we turned final, my feet were dancing on the rudder pedals and I couldn't believe the crab angle I had to crank in to stay on the center line of the runway. As we passed over the threshold I rolled in a bunch of right aileron, dropped the right wing, and started to juggle ailerons and rudder to keep her on the center line of the runway. It took almost full aileron and rudder, but I did it! She really boomed when we finally hit. It wasn't smooth, but I was pleased. Nothing had fallen off the plane. His hands had stayed in his lap the whole time, too.

"Take off and head west," I was told. The tower cleared us and away we went. As soon as we were clear, I was put through the grinder. Stalls, turns around a point, turns along a road, slow flight and everything else that Virgil and I had done. Then he pulled out the hood and I put it on with shaking hands.

After what Virgil had put me through, his tests were easy. Even with the turbulence, his unusual attitudes were a snap. I climbed, descended, did standard rate turns and flew on a VOR radial. He finally said that was enough instrument work and told me to head back to the airport. Then it happened.

As we turned final, he casually said, "Make this one a wheel landing."

"Oh God!" I thought. "Here it comes." I trimmed her for 65 mph adding 5 mph to help out the landing and started down. We passed over the threshold and I started to gingerly feel for the ground.

KER-SPRONNNNG! Yep, I'd found it. I tried to find it again.

KABOOM!! CLATTER!!! CRASH!! I was approaching a new personal record for bounces. His hands were still in his lap, but his palms were facing up and his spread out fingers were close to the wildly gyrating wheel.

Finally, he leaned over and snarled, "For cripes' sake, nail her down!"

I was getting tired of it, too, so on the next bounce I was able to keep her on the ground. I brought her to a stop and let out a big sigh of relief.

"Taxi to the ramp," he said.

I just flunked, I thought to myself. Virgil will have a stroke! We had only been up about 45 minutes and I was expecting a lot more action. I really felt bad. We got to the ramp and I turned the mags off. For about 30 seconds we just sat there like insects frozen in amber. The engine was making its ticking noises as it cooled down and the wind was whistling through the fuselage. He was scribbling furiously on his note pad. I was immersed in misery wondering how to tell Virgil that his perfect record had just been shattered.

He sighed and finally spoke. "Well, you did pretty good. Virgil trained you well. You really do need to work on your wheel landings though."

"You mean I passed?" I asked incredulously.

74

"Sure. Virgil always sends me students who have had it a lot worse than any check ride is going to be. Your instrument work was especially good. Come on into the office and I'll give you your temporary pilot's license. Your permanent one will be mailed to you later."

I was walking on air. It was the fulfillment of a long, impossible dream. I don't remember much about the flight back to Noah's. When I was on final I saw Sharon waiting beside the runway in our old 1971 terminally rusted-out Chevy van. I landed and taxied up to her.

She opened the right hand door of Tweety and asked, "Do I get to sleep with a Hot Fighter Pilot tonight?"

"Yep," I responded with a cheek splitting grin; "Three munths ago Ah couldn't even spell pileit and now I are one!"

She gave an excited squeal and laid a big old smackeroo on me. Then she pulled out a brand new, six foot long, white silk scarf from her purse.

"Congratulations, Ace!" she said as she wrapped the scarf around my neck. She jumped in the plane and buckled up. "Take me somewhere!"

* * *

That short flight was the prelude to many exciting adventures together.

First, we took Tweety Bird apart, trailered her home and in three months, over the winter, stripped and painted the fuselage, stripped and covered the wings, added wheel pants, gave her a pretty yellow and red color scheme, and installed a whole new interior. She was now a beauty that I could be proud of anywhere.

Sharon has become one heck of a navigator and has even taken a few flying lessons. Now, I think she could actually land the plane in a pinch. A whole new world had been opened up to us and we were ready to start. Life was full. I know I owe most of it to Virgil.

I thanked him by delivering two cases of his favorite soda pop to his house when I took the hood back to him. He's even honored me with a flight in his Swift. You can't get it any better than that. I have taken all my biennial check rides from him and he still throws everything at me like he did in our lessons. I showed him last time, though. After nine years, I have finally been able to get my wheel landings down to a gentle "chirp chirp" of the main gear on the runway. I think he is finally ready to say I am a pilot.

II

Now for the Fun Part

Togetherness

All kidding aside, folks.

I rolled over in bed and blearily squinted at the display on the bedside clock radio. Its blinking numbers told me it was 6 A.M. It was Saturday morning — I could sleep late if I wanted to. Gently rolling out of bed, trying not to disturb Sharon, I padded to the window to see what the weather looked like.

It was cloud-free. The dew glistened on the unmoving tree branches. It looked like the dawn of a perfect day for a fly-in breakfast.

But that meant I would have to get Sharon out of bed.

That woman loves to sleep. Getting her up is always a highly dangerous undertaking, and the chore has to be approached with care and cunning. Over the years I have developed two widely divergent methods. Both have their advantages and drawbacks. Both methods are extremely risky. A third option is to leave her behind when I go dark-thirty flying, but I can't do that, either. She loves to sleep but she loves to go flying even more. Therefore, I have to get her up. I just hope each time I do it that I will survive the ordeal. The really suspenseful time is that tenuous, fuzzy period when she's between deep sleep and bug-eyed awareness.

The Getting-Sharon-Out-of-the-Sack Ploy #1 is the quick and dirty method. It works only if I am fully awake and limbered up. It also helps if I am in a particularly suicidal frame of mind that morning. If a sufficiently tempting target of opportunity is peeking out from under the covers, I just give it a quick tickle and run like hell. This ploy never fails. She comes screaming straight up out of the bed shedding pillows and covers to the four winds, her claws and fangs bared. By the time she comes down I have made the stairs and am safe from pursuit. The words that come out of that sweet mouth! It's enough to make an old-time bosun's mate blush. I leave her a cup of coffee at the top of the stairs. Ploy #1 is useful if we are short of time and need to leave in less than ten minutes.

If time is not a factor and I don't feel the need of an early morning adrenaline rush, I use Ploy #2. I approach her like a veteran mountain man approaching a hibernating, nine-foot-tall silver-tipped Kodiak bear — with respect and caution. I waft the aroma of a cup of coffee under her nose from a safe distance so she can't hit me when she first strikes out. Alternately snarling and whining, she'll follow me downstairs, as I wave the tempting cup of java just out of her reach. I know then that the rest is downhill. She's awake and will be ready to go in twenty minutes.

This morning, there was enough time for Ploy #2. While she was throwing on her clothes, I got my flying equipment ready. My briefcase with logbooks, maps, flight calculator, and assorted other goods was placed in the car and by the time I had put some oil in and a jug of water to wash the windows of Tweety, Sharon was ready to go.

While driving to the airport, I mused on how times had changed since I took up flying. On any other Saturday before flying entered our lives, we would have lolled around in bed surrounded by snoring cats and dogs and finally rolled out around ten with nothing to do. Now, here we were at 6:30, heading out to the airport for breakfast at a picturesque little restaurant that would take us an hour and a half to drive to. In this case, the long drive was going to be replaced by a very pleasing thirty-minute flight.

We arrived at Noah's Ark at 6:45. I could see feverish action down in the hangar area. We untied the Tweety Bird and pushed her out of the hangar into the morning sunlight with only the crunching of her wheels on the gravel and the Bob White's calls breaking the morning stillness.

While Sharon cleaned the windshield, I gave Tweety her pre-flight. Tom's truck came around the end of the hangar. I heard a sudden burst of hysterical laughter and wondered at the cause. I understood when Tom and Carol drove down to our hangar. When he got out of his truck, my jaw dropped so far I heard it click. Tom was in a full tuxedo—ruffled shirt, black bow tie, striped pants and all. He looked elegant! I stared at him with my mouth hanging open. "Exactly what are you made up for?"

"You told me to dress," he said haughtily. I just shook my head. You have to know Tom to know that you will never know Tom. Standing next to him I felt like a hobo. He'd one-upped me again.

Our dauntless band gathered in a huddle like a real ragtag football team. We were just about ready to go. The only thing left was the world famous Preparation for Flight Group Check.

We had decided to do this after going to a local Experimental Aircraft Association meeting. The guest speaker really got our attention quick. After hearing from him about the FAA's enforcement policy and what they would do to you if *anything* was amiss in your papers or plane, we decided to be the most legal squeaky-clean pilots in the Greater Kansas City Metropolitan area. Those suckers were going to have to dig deep to find reasons to violate us! And we all know that if they really want to, they will find a reason. Whenever I run into an FAA guy it is always "Yes, sir! Right away, sir! Anything you say, sir! May I shine your shoes, sir?" etc., etc. I may look dumb (I may even *be* dumb) but I don't purposely go hunting trouble.

Doing a group preflight check this way helps you remember what you should. It went like this. Sharon read from the checklist and the rest of us responded like a Greek chorus:

"Fuel tanks full?"

"Check... Check... Check... Check."

Our voices echoed hollowly in the fog.

"Ear plugs?"

"Check... Check... Check... Check."

"Oil checked?"

"Check... Check." (snickers from the Rotax boys)

"Tires pumped up?"

"Check... Check... Check... Check."

"Bathroom?"

"Check... Check... Check... Drat!"

Tom went running off into the cornfield. We waited, shivering in silence, until he returned. The checklist was completed without further complications.

Sharon and I hopped into Tweety and buckled up. The C-85 muttered into life and we joined the line of planes taxiing slowly out to the runway. After a magneto check, carb heat check and control check, we took off and headed west climbing to 2300 feet. The six planes were in a very loose formation. (As far as the Noah's Ark International Dawn Patrol is concerned, formation flying is when all planes are heading in basically the same direction, at the same time, in the same state. Altitude has nothing to do with it. Other pilots have described us as a flock, not a formation.)

After we cleared the Kansas City Terminal Control Area, we all slowly climbed up to 4500 feet and pointed southwest, heading 240 degrees or thereabouts.

It was incredibly beautiful. The air was smooth as glass, and were it not for the soothing engine sounds, we could have been sitting in a luxury penthouse four thousand feet in the air. The sky was so clear we could see the grain elevators of Topeka etched against the razor-sharp horizon, fifty miles away. The golden, brown, and green fields of eastern Kansas rolled away into the far distance like an enormous patchwork quilt. The many lakes and ponds glistened in the early morning light like large scattered pools of molten silver and gold. Scattered patches of forests were mottled areas of crumpled green velvet.

Over the nose, a ribbon of pewter glistened on the horizon. It was Perry Reservoir, a nine mile long body of water located ten miles east of Topeka. One heck of a navigation landmark.

Sharon and I just sat there silently enjoying the exceptional view. We were racing through the air at ninety miles per hour but from 4500 feet above the ground it seemed like we and the other planes in the formation were suspended in space and the earth was crawling by slowly beneath us. It was only when we periodically flew along a road and passed a car that we got an impression of what our speed over the ground really was.

Every so often, I would feed in a few more hundred revs and creep up to Tom's left side so we could wave and smile at him and Carol. Then we would fall back and go back to enjoying the unobstructed view from our bird-like position above the earth.

**The golden, brown, and green fields of eastern Kansas rolled
away into the far distance like an enormous patchwork quilt.**

After a flight of about thirty-five minutes, we entered the pattern at Phillip Billard Field in Topeka. Following some discourse with the friendly folks in the control tower, we landed and parked our planes in front of one of the most unique restaurants in the Midwest.

The Eagle Squadron Restaurant was named after the American pilots who flew for the RAF in WWII before the United States entered the war. The entrance is dominated by an enormous Allison engine like the ones used in the P-40 War Hawk. The walls are sandbagged like the sides of a bunker and the ceiling is several opened parachutes. Camouflage netting, posters and pictures from WWII fight for space on the walls with bomb casings, machine gun belts and a plethora of assorted aviation memorabilia. All in all, it's a pilot's dream restaurant. The food is great, too.

Add the fact that you can eat breakfast with other fliers while you watch planes landing and taking off, and you are talking quality time.

We walked in, and as the people got a look at Tom, the whole place fell silent. You could hear eyeballs pop as the pilot clientele took in the ruffles on his shirt, the striped pants, the whole ensemble. Conversation slowly resumed, but it was a little subdued.

Every time a plane landed on the runway in front of the restaurant, forks stopped in midair as we all watched the landing and commented on the pilot's skill in regaining contact with terra-firma, the plane's paint job, and any other thing that captured our fancy.

After a leisurely, delicious meal, we once more formed up and started the trek back home to Noah's Ark. It was a repeat of the flight to the restaurant. Pure enjoyment.

This is what pleasure flying is all about, and Sharon and I love it. No frantic schedule to meet, no phones ringing and demanding our attention, no kids, no hassle. Simply a feeling of peace and tranquility that does wonders for the soul.

I don't need to mention that considering the cost of the plane, hangar rent, fuel, oil, insurance, taxes and many other little miscellaneous items, the price of a little breakfast adventure like that is probably about fifty dollars. Is it worth it? You bet! Every penny and then some! Talk to any pilot and spouse and you'll get the same story.

We have enjoyed many such flights over the years. The sale of the Tweety Bird (which I'll tell you about later) ended all that. Until we were able to replace Tweety with another two-seater, I could no longer have Sharon beside me on my many adventures. That was a serious blow to my flying pleasure.

It was losing the Tweety Bird that made me realize the truth in what many other pilots over the years have told me. Pleasure flying is a much more enjoyable pastime when it can be shared with someone who enjoys it as much as you do. That's one of the reasons you see so many married couples up at Oshkosh dedicated to the same engrossing pastime.

Introducing a newcomer to light plane flying is a very enjoyable experience, too. Tweety and I have provided many first small-plane rides to people who are frequent flyers on major airlines. They all respond the same way to the takeoff, the flight, and the landing: complete amazement and enjoyment. Their perspective from out of an airliner's window cruising at 35,000 feet and going 550 miles per hour is totally unlike the scene from 2000 feet at 95 miles per hour. Suddenly the fun is back. Not only can they enjoy the view, they can see where they are going. They become part of the living landscape instead of an intruder up in the lifeless heights so far above the earth. They can see the cows, kids playing ball, and cars scooting along the ground.

It's an emotional, inspirational high not enjoyed by many other mortals.

Weather!

"Do a 180 and Run Like Hell!"

I knew we were in deep doo-doo. What made it worse was that this time it wasn't even my fault! This wasn't supposed to happen! I'd had a weather briefing and had even filed a flight plan! I stared glumly through the rain-drenched windshield of the Tweety Bird while threads of panic galloped wildly through my veins. Not only were we lost, we were in rapidly deteriorating weather.

Sharon, our daughter Tricia, and I were returning from a trip down to Dauphin Island off the coast of Mobile, Alabama. The Tweety Bird was full to the brim with Sharon and me in the front seat and my 60-pound daughter crammed in the back seat with the 15 pounds of luggage the CG figures allowed.* We were heading for Springfield, Missouri. The briefer at the Memphis FSS had forecast "3000 scattered, 8000 broken, good VFR all the way to Springfield, Missouri."

It had been a perfect vacation. We had flown down to Dauphin

---

* The CG, or center of gravity, is the measured point on an airplane at which the aircraft would balance or hang level if it were suspended. This measurement is very important, since having a CG too far to the rear or too far forward would make the aircraft unmanageable in the air. Pilots must load fuel, people, and baggage within the CG "envelope" as specified in the aircraft's operations manual.

Island, located five miles out in the Gulf of Mexico south of Mobile, Alabama. We landed at Brookley Field in Mobile to fuel up and took time out to go see the battleship *Alabama*.

The only embarrassing note had been when I got lost again, on the ground for a change, trying to taxi to the FBO at Brookley Field. The tower finally had to send a car out to get me. The field had been a WWII training base and was so big that sitting on the ground in the Tweety Bird, I couldn't see where to go. The controllers in the tower were very patient and understanding between guffaws.

After leaving Mobile, we started the five mile odyssey over water to the island's airport with its 3000-foot runway.

The bridge between Mobile and the Island had been destroyed by a hurricane and the only way to get to the island was either by plane or ferry. Since massive reconstruction was going on, the ferry was restricted to island inhabitants and construction workers. On the other hand, flying to the island was unrestricted.

We had secured reservations at a small motel which had stayed open after the storm. It was just across the street from a little seafood restaurant and only a two-minute walk from the gulf.

For five days, Sharon and I had sat on the deserted beach or tumbled and played in the surf with Trish.

We rose early each day and watched the sunrise as we ate breakfast on the beach. We walked for miles along the beach collecting shells and sunburn. At night we ate at the little restaurant and slept the sleep of the truly exhausted. In all that time, we saw only five other people. It was idyllic.

* * *

I should have remembered how fast convective storms can build in the south on a hot, muggy, summer day. A line of thunderstorm cells unexpectedly formed up over the highway I was following northwest from Memphis to Jonesboro. I turned north to try and fly around the cells but another cell formed ahead of me. It was time to give up. Virgil had always told me that the smartest thing to do when encountering bad weather was to "make a 180-degree turn and run like hell!"

I turned back toward Memphis but the developing weather had closed in behind me. Lightning was dancing on the southern horizon like the devil's picket fence. I pushed the panic button down and locked it in the on position. My pucker factor went up to 8. (10 is ground loop.) South, East, and North were out. I turned southwest toward the only semi-clear area I could see. The rain was hitting the windshield so hard we could hear it over the sound of the engine.

It took 45 hour-long minutes of snaking around and between isolated cells before we saw sunlight on the western horizon. Once we were finally clear of the cells I picked up a northern compass heading and thrashed onward into the unknown looking for landmarks. I wasn't even sure what sectional we were on by then. All we could see were winding brown sluggish streams and rice fields. Lost again! Just once I would like to make a flight longer than 50 miles and not get lost.

Sweetums went to high pucker and started her usual You Big Stupid Idiot routine. I don't know why she always gets so excited when this happens. She knows that sooner or later I'll find out where we are. The only thing that really distracts me when we're lost is the rattle and clatter of her well-worn rosary beads and the plaintive Hail Marys from the right hand seat.

Tricia snored peacefully away in the back seat. Ah, the trusting innocence of the young!

Soon, just like I knew it would, a string of power lines glistened in the sun. I aligned us with them and we found where we were as we thundered on to Springfield, and finally landed after another interesting flight.

Sharon and I went into the Flight Service Station to cancel my flight plan. I just happened to mention to the briefer the rough weather we had encountered and the convoluted detours we were forced to take to maintain VFR.

Some drunk-with-power young FAA buck hanging by his toes from the ceiling overheard my tale of woe, unfurled his wings, and flapped over to the counter. He interrupted me and the sympathetic briefer I was talking to and started to give me the third degree about flying into the weather we had encountered.

"Hey you there!" he pompously barked. "Are you instrument rated?" The overhead fluorescent lights glistened on his dripping fangs.

"No," I said. "And as a matter of fact, neither is my wife, my daughter, or my plane."

He licked his thin lips like a hungry jackal sighting a helpless quarry. His red, beady little close-set piggy eyes got a ravenous gleam in them.

"Well, you should know better than to fly into instrument conditions when you aren't qualified." he blustered. "That's a violation of FARs." He was already cheerfully filling out countless violation forms in his malevolent, vindictive little mind.

Something inside me snapped. I looked at him with bloodshot eyes and growled, "Hey, bucko! Number one, I maintained VFR for the whole trip. Number two, if you want to bitch at someone, talk to the briefer who told me it was going to be 3000 scattered, 8000 broken, VFR all the way!" I nailed him with my self-righteous glare. "I filed a flight plan and received a weather briefing just before I left Memphis. It was all recorded over the phone." I threw the notes from the briefing and my flight plan on the counter in front of him. (I would like to say at this time that the briefing I had been given was probably as accurate as possible at the time it was given. I know as well as anybody how fast weather in the Midwest can change.)

He looked up from the flight plan notes into my glaring, red-veined eyes and outraged face. He knew that he was looking at a man on the ragged edge.

Then there was a low, sinister, blood-chilling snarl from behind me. Uh-oh! I'd heard that heart-stopping sound before. Mr. Obnoxious peeked around behind me and saw Sweetums strapping on her climbing spikes, preparatory to starting her ascent up his frame. I quickly got out of the line of fire. This peckerwood had just stepped into some serious guano. He was dog meat now. He'd picked on the wrong wife's husband. Gleefully, I stood back to watch the execution.

Sharon is a petite 5'3" 115-pound, soft-spoken, even-tempered, freckle-faced, cute-as-a-bug sweetie pie. But during the first three months of our marriage, I found out that when you cross her and light her fuse, you have definitely fouled the nest. When the explosion occurs, she's suddenly nine feet tall and completely covered with fangs, claws, and hair. Godzilla himself wouldn't mess with her.

Mr. Self-Importance looked at her infuriated face and judiciously chose retreat. Swirling an invisible cape around himself, he indignantly slithered off searching for less belligerent prey. It was a perspicacious decision. He lived to bully student pilots another day. I threw Sharon some raw meat to calm her down. The guttural snarling subsided.

There was a low, sinister, blood-chilling snarl from behind me.

The old hand who had been giving me my briefing grinned at the departing FAAer's back and said, "Don't mind him, he's been spring-loaded in the teed-off position ever since he got here. He's just out to make a name for himself." This briefer and I had a real nice chat and he gave me an excellent, accurate briefing for the final leg back to dear old Kansas City.

By the way, in eleven years of flying, that rude young man was the only person out of hundreds and hundreds of FAA, FSDO, tower, approach, departure and FSS personnel to give me a hard time. Everyone else has bent over backward to be helpful to me and has never laughed at my dumb questions. (I do have to admit that some of the weather briefers have given me some strange looks. I still can't read those damnable weather strips while someone is watching me.)

The flight from Springfield to Kansas City was smooth and uneventful. We didn't get lost. (Rand-McNally, Highway 71 North.) When I was making my logbook entries concerning the leg from Memphis to Springfield, I wrote in "Weather." That said it all.

The Bent Prop

The $500 flying lesson.

It was one of those balmy August evenings that made you glad to be alive. The air was dead calm and the sun, hanging low on the western horizon, was casting a seductive, hazy golden-yellow glow over the river bottoms. The sultry heat of the day had subsided and it was just warm enough to make you glad you weren't exercising. I was sitting with the rest of the rail birds, watching the traffic take off and land at Noah's Ark International Airport. After a hard day's flying, nothing was quite as relaxing as reclining there, with my chair leaned back against the office, sharing outrageous lies and boasts with the rest of the guys while sipping on a hearty bottle of diet cola.

This was not the type of crowd that you would find gathered in a trendy Manhattan bar frequented by skinny, effete, chinless, sallow-complexioned, Madison-Avenue-type Yuppies. This group was engaged in macho, sweaty, hairy-chested male bonding at its best. The dialogue consisted of dirty jokes, FAA bashing, and derogatory comments about any absent pilot's lack of flying skill.

As each plane in the pattern turned final to land, the group would fall silent. Everyone would stop whatever he was doing and analyze the pilot's prowess in regaining contact with old mother earth. If the landing was a greaser, nothing would be said, and the conversations would resume. If, however, the plane ended up bounding down the runway to the accompaniment of screeching tires and smoking brakes, the laughter and comments were loud, pungent, and scathing.

I had long ago deduced that a landing that kept this crowd quiet was the greatest accolade you could be given as a pilot. If you really bounced one in, it was in your best interest not to join the group after you had put your bird away. It was bad for your ego. I didn't even like to think of the entertainment I had given to the grateful gallery back when I was a student pilot. Several times I judiciously took the back road out of the airport, so I wouldn't have to drive past the crowd and listen to the shouts of derision.

Now, I was a veteran pilot and inordinately proud of the several hundred hours I had laboriously built up in my logbook. I was even more proud of the fact that now I could sometimes walk up to the crowd at the shack after putting Tweety back in the barn and join in the conversations without having to put up with five minutes of caustic analysis of my landing(s).

We were all sitting there, engaged in our usual suave and witty repartee, when a pretty little yellow and blue Taylorcraft made a fly-by down the runway. We all recognized the plane as one belonging to an airline pilot who lives across the river in Leavenworth, Kansas. During his work week, he pilots 767s and other heavy iron over the ocean. On his days off, he jumps into his 1946 Taylorcraft and hops around the area.

The plane completed a tight circuit around the pattern and lined up for a landing. As it crossed the threshold, the pilot leveled her out and touched her down on the right wheel. He then gently picked her up and rolled her on the left wheel. This dance was repeated down the runway several times until he was at about mid-field.

Then, delicately as a ballerina tip-toeing on the stage, he set her down on her main wheels and rolled, tail high, by the intersection. As we all watched silently, he slowly braked the plane to a stop, with the tail still in the air. The crowd was awestruck at this display of skill.

Then he slowly lowered the tail to the ground.

A reverent, whispered "Damn" was the only comment from that super-critical, hard-bitten bunch.

I watched all this with narrowed eyes. I COULD DO THAT!! I knew I could. All I had to do was practice.

The next several mornings I was out at oh-dark-thirty practicing my wheel landings. I was too smart to try that wheel-to-wheel dance, but I thought I was good enough to learn the stop-with-tail-high bit. After about two weeks of furtive practice, I was ready for the final test. Tom, my partner in many disastrous escapades, wanted to go flying with me, and I decided to impress the heck out of him and the rail birds at the same time. We took off and I started my crosswind turn to make a close-in pattern.

"Tom," I said during the turn, "I'm going to show you how good I'm getting at wheel landings. You just watch this." His eyebrows went up questioningly, but he said nothing as I completed the pattern and turned onto a short final.

As we crossed over the threshold, I started to juggle the yoke and throttle while feeling for the ground. One wheel squeaked on and then the other. So far, so good. Then I eased the yoke forward to keep the tail up and started to gently feel with the brakes and the throttle for the precise balance between the two to keep the tail up and slow down the roll-out at the same time. As we rolled down the runway I could see the crowd at the office watching.

By the time we got abeam of the audience, I had Tweety almost stopped. Then — and here is where you might hear two different stories — the tail slowly started to rise. I maintain that the brakes locked up or the wind suddenly died, and Tom contends that my head was up my rear and locked in position. Whichever version you believe, she started over onto her nose. I yanked the throttle closed, but it was too late. She was committed. We were going to end up with our butt in the air. The engine was at full idle when the prop finally bit into the runway.

CLATTER CLATTER CLATTER. I couldn't believe the racket the prop made as it chewed its way into the asphalt. Tom said later that all he could see were hundred-dollar bills flying by the window.

When it was all over, the Tweety Bird was standing on her nose, in disgrace, in the middle of the runway. Tom and I were sitting there in the cockpit, staring at the runway from a range of about five feet. I still had the yoke back against the stop. (Why, I don't know. I think I was still hoping she would come back down.) Tom's hands were a blur as he was turning off every switch on the instrument panel. Then we just perched there, frozen in time, silently watching the gas from the wing

I couldn't believe the racket the prop made
as it chewed its way into the asphalt.

tanks run over the windshield. It seemed that an hour passed as we sat there.

I turned to look at Tom. He looked at me. His eyes were bugged out like a tromped-on toad. Suddenly he bellowed, "LET'S GET OUT OF HERE!" We threw open the doors and catapulted out onto the runway.

By then the crowd had already gathered and a spirited discussion erupted as to how to get the plane back on her feet. The tail wheel was waaaaay up there in the air and we couldn't get a hand on it, even using the rickety ladder the airport owned. The plane was too heavy to lift at the nose, so a rope was found and we tried to lasso the tail wheel. To most of the mob that had gathered, it was downright hilarious. But not to me. It looked like a drunken rodeo. Finally someone got it roped, accompanied by appreciative roars from the now enormous crowd. It was simple then to pull her back down onto her feet.

She was a sorry sight. The carburetor heat box was smashed up into the cowling. The last three inches of the prop tips bent back in pretty curves. You could see where the asphalt had carved out little grooves in the metal. At least the cowling was untouched; that was the saving grace. I sorrowfully pushed her back into her hangar.

We borrowed a wrench from Noah and were able to pull the mangled prop off the engine. I headed home to get my tools, taking the prop with me, and left it standing against the front of the garage – not a wise move as later events proved – and then went back to the airport.

Meanwhile, Tom drove home and got his dial indicator and came back just as I finished pulling the ruined heat box off the intake manifold. We hooked up the dial indicator and checked the crankshaft runout. It was well within new engine tolerances. Thank the heavens!! I didn't have to pull the engine off and break it down. The prop had hit the runway only three times at idle throttle setting. We found all three grooves in the asphalt. By this time Tom, my dad, and about five other A&Ps were gathered around the scene and offering advice and criticism.

Just about then, my rusty old 1975 Honda Civic tore around the corner of the hangar on two wheels in a cloud of dust. Sharon jumped out, spotted me and said, "Are you all right?"

"Sure," I replied.

She gathered steam and started to yell. "THEN WHY DIDN'T

YOU LEAVE A NOTE, YOU BIG STUPID IDIOT?" The crowd scattered. "DO YOU KNOW WHAT I THOUGHT WHEN I CAME UP THE DRIVEWAY AND SAW THAT MANGLED PROP!!??" she screamed. She seemed upset.

I shuffled my feet and looked at the ground. "I'm sorry, dear," I apologized in my best little boy voice. "I was just worried about getting back down here and checking out the crankshaft."

She glowered at me a little while longer and finally, in a low menacing voice, asked the burning question. "How much is this latest little disaster going to cost me?"

I didn't know. I didn't want to know. I told her that. By then, some of the A & Ps in the crowd had taken pity on me and were reassuring her that the engine wasn't hurt, the prop would be easy to get repaired at a local prop shop, and all I had to replace was the heat box. They were right. The final bill was about $500 for everything. Still, it was one hell of an expensive flying lesson. I learned then not to show off when I didn't know what I was doing. I'm still catching flak about this incident and it happened years ago. Dumb acts will always come back to haunt you.

"PUT HER DOWN!"

This is no drill!

While the mangled prop was in the prop shop getting a facelift, I had nothing to do. Too broke to rent a plane (I discovered real quick that if you own a plane, you won't have any spare cash to go around), I spent my free afternoons sitting on a bench down at the airport trying to mooch a ride from anybody who would take me.

I sat there masochistically amidst the rail birds and endured an abundant helping of razzing and caustic remarks about my piloting skills, along with many innuendoes and outright insults. I was thanked countless times for being considerate enough to do it right in front of the office — the grateful crowd hadn't even had to stand to see the exhibition. As the afternoons wore on, the crowd would grow. Pretty soon someone would think of a hilarious remark reflecting on my flying skill. At least they thought it was hilarious. While the braying laughter was echoing back from the hills, I would just smile a sick smile. A smart individual would have left, but I wanted to fly. And taking all the witty abuse was cathartic. I resolved then and there to never again do anything dumb in front of a crowd.

Anyway, a few days after the nose-over, I was sitting there hoping that someone would offer to take me for a ride when Tom drove up. At that time he was the proud owner of a beautiful polished aluminum

1946 Cessna 120. He called it The Silver Slug. (Tom is not a roman-
ticist.)

Tom looked at me sitting there with a wistful look on my face and
said, "Hey, Crash!" (A roar of laughter from the crowd.) "You want to
go flying with a good pilot?" (More laughter.)

I nodded my head eagerly and leaped to my feet. "You bet! Let's
go."

We drove down to the hangar where the Slug was straining at her
anchors. I was so pathetically grateful for a chance to fly that when
Tom imperiously ordered, "Perform the preflight, slave! I'm going to
go talk with the real pilots," I meekly swallowed my pride and started
to untie the bird. While I was doing this, he walked back to the crowd,
where lies flowed in a rushing torrent.

I always start and finish my preflights at the dip stick. I checked the
oil level on the right side. Closed that cowl flap, then checked the
engine compartment on the port side. Then I checked the static port,
kicked the left tire, checked the pitot tube, port aileron hinges, port
gas tank for water, port elevator hinges, rudder hinges, tail wheel,
starboard elevator hinges, starboard gas tank, starboard aileron hinges, kicked the right tire and ended back up where I started.

"YOUR PRE-FLIGHT IS COMPLETE, CAPTAIN GLAESER,
YOUR SUPREME ROYAL HIGHNESS, MAJESTY, SIR!" I
screamed.

"IT'S ABOUT TIME, SLAVE!" he screamed back. Tom
sauntered around the plane giving her a cursory once-over and we got
in. After the Before-Start checklist was gone over, he gave her a few
shots of prime, graciously allowed me to holler,"CLEAR PROP!" and
pulled the starter T-handle.

As we waddled out to the taxiway, we passed the crowd and they all
stood up and solemnly made the sign of the cross. I gave them a return
sign of a different nature.

We got to the end of the taxiway and went through the Before-
Takeoff checklist. Everything looked good. After a check for traffic,
Tom turned her onto the runway and firewalled the throttle.

She lifted off sweetly and Tom turned west over the river bottoms.
It was beautiful! The ponds and lakes glistened against the green and
brown fields. I had forgotten how great it was to just sit and look out at
the world. I sat there with my nose pressed against the window and

watched the scenery slowly unwind beneath me. It was just swell! When you are the pilot you are always looking for traffic and watching the engine gauges (that is, if you're a good pilot) and don't really have time to just *enjoy*! I just sat there and vegetated. Talk about stress relief! This was great!

We had been in the air for about five minutes. I was gazing down at the tranquil view when Tom suddenly screamed, "AAAUUUG-GGHHH!! MY GOD! WE'VE GOT TO PUT HER DOWN!"

I jerked bolt upright in the seat and looked at his pointing finger. He was gesturing at the oil temperature gauge. The needle was resting on the 230-degree mark. (Normal operating temperature was about 180 and the *never exceed* temp was 210!) Uh-oh. I tapped the gauge, hoping the reading was erroneous. It was — it jumped to 235 degrees. Tom pulled the power back to full idle and we started down. The oil temperature went up to 240 degrees. Strangely, the oil *pressure* needle was still within the green arc.

I'd like to be able to say that during all the excitement that followed, we were like the handsome young pilots in TOP GUN, speaking in low, deep, calm voices and making little macho pilot jokes. Alas, it's not true. Our voices were high and squeaky like a speeded-up recording of two 175-pound mice with their tails caught in a trap.

We were over large, flat fields that stretched to the horizon. Tom was frantically looking for a suitable spot to land when I remembered that we were close to a grass strip that belongs to a TWA heavy iron pilot. I looked out the window and saw the runway. It was well within gliding distance. Oil temperature, 235 degrees.

I tried to point out the strip to Tom. I was so excited that when I tried to explain where it was, the only thing that came out of my mouth was gurgling gibberish. My mind was working at Mach 2 but my mouth was frozen in horror.

I tried again. More gurgles. I took a deep breath, pointed, and shrieked, "STRIP!! STRIP!! STRIP!!"

Tom looked with wild eyes to where I was pointing and screamed back, "WHERE??!! WHERE??!! WHERE??!!"

I frantically pointed again with a shaking finger and screeched, "THERE!! THERE!! THERE!!"

"I STILL CAN'T SEE IT!"

I grabbed his head with both hands and pointed his nose at it. "IT'S

RIGHT THERE!" I shook his head to emphasize the point. Why couldn't he see it?

"I STILL CAN'T SEE THE BLEEPING THING!!" he shouted.

"BLEEP BLEEP DOUBLE-BLEEP!!!!" I bellowed, "IT'S RIGHT THERE!!" I emphatically pointed again. Tom still couldn't see it. I tried to use a pencil to point it out to him and promptly poked him in the eye with it.

"BLEEEEEEP!!" Tom screamed and sat there with one eye squeezed shut, tears leaking out in a stream. His other eye was blinking like a frog in a hail storm. His language would have shriveled an angel's wings.

He gave me a vicious shot in the ribs with his elbow and screamed, "POINT HER AT IT!" I grabbed the controls and kicked the Slug around until she was lined up on a long, easy-glide, final approach. Tom saw the strip and grabbed the yoke. "I'VE GOT IT!"

He greased her on one third of the way down the strip and we slowly rolled to a stop; then he killed the engine. We both just sat there for a few minutes practicing deep breathing exercises while we tried to relax. The adrenalin rush was still roaring in my ears like a pounding surf.

Finally, we got out and walked around to look at the engine. Tom almost fainted. The anti-bird-nest plates were still in place over the engine air intakes. He had used clear plastic sheets to block the intakes so birds couldn't get in and build one of their feathered condominiums. I hadn't even noticed them during my preflight.

Tom said a few choice polysyllabic words, ripped the offending pieces of plastic out of the holes and threw them back into the plane. I unreeled a litany of apologies but he interrupted me.

"Don't apologize. It's my fault," he said. "It's my plane. I'm the pilot in command. I knew those suckers were in there. I should have done the preflight. Besides that, those things shouldn't have been made out of clear plastic. Forget it."

He thought for a minute. "Just one more thing. Don't tell those jokers back at the airport about this. I don't want to go through what you have been going through."

We lay in the cool grass under the wing and waited for the oil temperature to go down. It took a long time. We didn't say much. We were both lost in thought. What should you really do in situations like that? Fly on, hoping the engine doesn't seize until you find a "decent" emergency field, or immediately put her down anywhere? We still haven't decided, but have talked about it a lot.

After the engine cooled down, we carefully flew back to Noah's. The oil pressure and temperature were normal for the flight back. We immediately changed the oil and closely examined the oil screen and the old oil. No chunks of metal... no damage. We were lucky.

* * *

Tom and I learned a lot from that experience. Since then, we have never let anyone else do a preflight on our planes. That has browned off a few other pilots who had thought they were doing us a favor. It wasn't that we didn't trust them. We had learned. When it's your plane, you know what to check. Since it's your butt up there on the line, *don't trust anybody*! Do your own preflight. If I am going to go flying with another pilot, I always silently follow him around as he does his preflight and make sure that he doesn't forget anything important. You'd be surprised at how many high-time pilots will get careless and forget some major item. Flying is one sport where you can never become complacent or lazy. Just as soon as you start to think you know it all, you are sure to get bitten.

Caution, Mother on Board!

It was a time to lie.

"Aw, come on, Mom," I pleaded. "Let me take you on one short flight — just to show you how she handles." I had been trying to get my mother to go flying with me ever since I got my private pilot's certificate. So far, no luck. She wouldn't go. Her response had always been the same.

"Listen here, Dickie-boy," she'd say. (I'm 46 years old and Momma still calls me Dickie-boy.) "You add three more engines to that heap, show in-flight movies, and have a stewardess serving me a martini and then I'll *think* about it. Besides that, the last time you landed, you stood that pile of junk up on its nose. I'm not going and that's that. End of discussion."

Undaunted, I kept trying to talk her into it, and over the months I could see she was wearing down. Sharon and my dad were also working on her. Every time I brought them back from someplace exotic like Topeka, St. Joseph, or Lawrence, we would regale her with stories about how great the flight had been and how beautiful the western Missouri scenery was. And nobody had died yet. After three months, she was starting to waver.

It was time to move in with the argument that finally convinced her to go: I told her about the Eagle Squadron Restaurant. She finally gave in and said I could take her for one of my famous breakfast flights.

I chose a Saturday morning that was blessed with light winds, twenty-mile visibility, and temperatures in the 70's—flawless flying weather. I cleaned up the Tweety Bird and checked everything I could in preparation for this first, most important flight. I knew that if this trip went well, she would go on many more. I wanted everything to be perfect.

I picked Mom up and drove her down to Noah's. I showed her how I did a preflight and explained everything that I was doing. Mom climbed into the passenger seat, a little pale but determined to go though with it. Besides that, I had promised to buy her breakfast and she would go though the tortures of the damned to eat out.

I had her read off the Before-Start checklist and I responded to each of her comments with "Roger" or "Check" just to show her how professional I was at this flying stuff. Everything was "Go." I had her scream out "CLEAR PROP!" and pulled on the starting handle.

As we taxied out, I gave a running commentary on everything I was doing just to keep her from thinking about what *she* was doing.

Reaching the end of the taxiway, I braked Tweety to a stop, and had Mom read off the Before-Takeoff checklist. We checked the mags, set the altimeter, worked the controls, checked carburetor heat and looked for traffic. Rolling onto the active, I eased the throttle in all the way. We accelerated down the runway and lifted off into the glassy smooth air. It was just swell! Mom was already commenting on how pretty it was. "Look how far we can see!" She said all the neat things people say when they first take off and get a couple of hundred feet of altitude.

We reached 300 feet above the ground and it was time to make the crosswind turn. I picked up the mike with a practiced flourish, "Mom, I'm going to advise any traffic in the area that we are going to depart to the west." I really wanted to keep her informed as to what was happening.

I keyed the mike and started to speak. At this point, the perfect flight suddenly went south. The ammeter needle pegged itself to the left side showing a sudden massive discharge. Simultaneously, there was a brilliant white flash, followed by a shower of sparks from under the instrument panel where the radio power supply was located. An instant later, a dense cloud of evil-smelling black smoke gushed out

There was a brilliant white flash, followed by a shower of sparks from under the instrument panel.

from under the instrument panel. This was not at all the way I had planned this flight.

My sweet little old momma, her hair standing straight up, screamed, jerked bolt upright in her seat and yelled, "WHAT THE *BLEEP* WAS THAT??!!"

I looked over at her in shock. Those sweet, saintly lips had just uttered the prime curse word of them all! Her delivery, let alone her choice of words, left little doubt that she had become somewhat dismayed when the smoke spewed out in her face. She wasn't alone, either. She never knew that the only reason I didn't scream right along with her was I was busy spitting plastic. When the shower of sparks sprinkled itself on my lap, I had taken a big bite out of the microphone.

Now, you've got to see this from my point of view. Here I thought my beloved plane had just blown up in my face and, at the same time, my saintly little old soft-spoken momma had blurted out the type of word that always got me a vigorous tooth-brushing with laundry soap when I used it. I had to calm this woman down, and at the same time, I had to get this smoking bird back on the ground... QUICK! My agile brain darted to a familiar solution – I lied.

"Heh, heh, heh. Oh, that's nothing, Mom," I said while frantically turning off every electrical switch on the panel and throwing the master switch. "We just blew the fuse on the radio. It's no big deal. Happens all the time. We're going to have to land while I replace it." I cranked Tweety around in a 45-degree bank and entered a tight pattern to get back to the field as quickly as possible. Reaching around behind my seat, I snatched the fire extinguisher that I carried and handed it to Mom.

"Would you mind holding this for me?" I said, with a shaky voice and a sickly smile.

"What the bleep is this for?" she asked, in a shrill voice. She still didn't have a very tight grip on her vocabulary. I didn't know her eyes could open so wide. It was time for big lie number two.

"Oh, didn't you know?" I stammered. "It's just standard operating procedure for the passenger to hold a fire extinguisher when a plane is making a landing approach. Just keep it aimed at the instrument panel and squeeze the trigger hard if I tell you to. OK?"

She had that sucker in a death grip so tight that from that moment, it took on a noticeable hourglass shape. She was waving it around just like Marshall Dillon when he was getting ready to shoot the bad guys. I just hoped she didn't activate it while I was in the middle of the landing flare.

The pattern and landing probably only took about two minutes but it seemed like two years. The smoke was almost gone now and only the intense smell of charred electrical components remained. I taxied Tweety back to her hangar. There, I made an exhaustive search for replacement fuses, being very careful not to look where I knew they were. I couldn't find any.

"Well rats, Mom. I can't find any fuses and we can't go to Topeka without a radio. We'll just have to do it again some other day." I put Tweety back in her hangar. Then we went to breakfast... by car.

The old Narco was cooked well-done and wasn't worth repairing. It was pulled out and a "newer" used solid-state radio was installed in the bird at an unbelievably obnoxious price.

I was so casual about the whole episode that to this day I think she thought a cloud of acrid smoke boiling out from under the instrument panel was an everyday occurrence when I went flying.

Mom did finally get her breakfast flight. It truly went great. We have taken a lot of flights over the past ten years. The only hard part has been remembering to hand her the fire extinguisher as we enter the pattern to land. She still thinks it is standard operating procedure.

Annual Time

"Quick! Another Band-Aid!"

Hot, salty, stinging sweat was running into my eyes. I was breathing in short puffs and hoping another cramp would not hit. "Please, oh please... " I moaned. "Legs, don't fail me now." I was curled up like a worm that had been dropped on a hot rock. The temperature in my own private little piece of hell had to be at least 140 degrees. My shirt and pants were soaked from sweat and I was starting to smell like a road-kill skunk.

I was scrunched up, facing backwards, in the tail cone of the Tweety Bird, performing my usual trial by fire — the annual inspection. Ah, the fond memories those yeasty little experiences bring back. Until I had bought my plane, I didn't know what an annual inspection was. Now, a veteran of ten such tribulations, I am still not sure that I really needed the knowledge.

Every aircraft has to have an annual. The FAA says so. An annual inspection is a trying time for an owner. Your plane is basically taken apart, examined meticulously by an unsympathetic, eagle-eyed, just-looking-for-something-to-be-wrong inspector — and then, if you're lucky and nothing is wrong, put back together and you get to fly it another year. Usually, an annual will leave you with a lot flatter wallet and a heartily hacked-off spouse. There are some options open to you, however. If you are so inclined, you can do a lot of the work yourself and save a bundle of money.

My dad bullied me through my first annual. He made me clean that plane up like she was Air Force One and the President was going to go fly in it the next day. When I mistakenly brought that to his attention I was unceremoniously told, "Shut up, Boy! If my butt is going flying in this junk heap, this annual, and all the rest, are going to be done right!" I slunk back to work. He just sat there in his folding chair, sipping on iced tea, barking instructions and repeating, "That's not good enough. *Do it over!*" When I finally got something safety-wired or cleaned to his satisfaction, I knew it had been done right.

So, every annual, I would laboriously crawl back into the cramped little sewer pipe that the rear fuselage of the Tweety Bird resembled, to wash the inside of the fuselage and check every bulkhead, rivet, screw and cable. I would never admit it to my dad, but he was right. The annual is your chance to make sure all the little things that have not been looked at all year long are in good condition.

I wiped down all the control cables with a rag soaked in LPS-2 to clean and lubricate them, while at the same time checking them for any loose strands. I learned the first time I did an annual that you always use a rag to check control cables. Just running your hand down a cable is a foolish thing to do. You would be amazed at how far one of those little strands will go into your fingers. A couple of times I was afraid to look because I thought it was going to be all the way through the injured member.

All the cables were clean and running free. Now it was time to turn around and check the aileron cross-over cable where it passed from side-to-side at the top of the fuselage. For a skinny jockey, it would have been no problem. For an out-of-shape, slightly rotund, six-foot-tall specimen of macho masculinity, it was a definite challenge. The tail cone is about three feet in diameter, littered with cables running along the bottom, and has bulkheads scattered in it, so there is no place where you can rest your feet and rear comfortably. It is one of life's greater thrills to get a charley horse in your leg while crammed in the back of a fuselage on a steamy August afternoon.

Sharon always accompanies me on these adventures so she can hand me tools and Band-Aids as I labor like a damned soul in the black hole of Calcutta. The first time I got a cramp, even she was amazed at the way the plane rocked on its gear legs as I thrashed around back there. She was also very impressed at the intensity and level of cursing. She said it was a new high.

I got turned around and was just getting ready to reach up and oil the pulley that the aileron cross-over cable runs through when, like a stroke of lighting, the first cramp of the day hit. I immediately started to flail around, trying to attain a position where I could straighten out my leg and ease the excruciating agony. As I did, I started to lose my balance and reached out to brace myself on the fuselage bottom. I screwed up bad. I grabbed a turnbuckle and a stray end from the safety-wiring on the turnbuckle sunk into my thumb at least three inches, with a searing flash of pain. I rocked back and forth, keening in agony.

"OH GOSH! OH DEAR!! OH GOLLY!!!" I screamed. (The actual language I used escapes me at the moment.) I was bleeding all over my newly cleaned fuselage. This had to stop! Nothing gets an inspector more suspicious than bloodstains in an airplane.

"SHARON!" I screamed. "BAND-AID!... ECONOMY SIZE!... QUICK!!!" Like the well-trained wife she is, she sprang into action. Her hand appeared in the small crawl hole between the cabin and fuselage rear holding a bandage. What a girl! She is so used to me doing this that she can read a book while handing me tools, safety wire, Band-Aids and anything else I scream for.

Whimpering as I sucked on my lacerated thumb, I contemplated my current state of affairs. I was two minutes away from heat stroke. I had a cramp in my leg. I was drenched in sweat. I was working in conditions that would be called cruel and unusual punishment by any shyster lawyer in the civilized world. I was bleeding freely... I was also happy as a clam. You see, I was working on my own plane. If you love flying like I do, you would put up with a lot more. Stripping paint off a fuselage, outside, in the winter... that's a different story. I'd never do that again.

I have never operated from what you would call a big airport. The fields I fly out of are usually deserted a major portion of the day. Only on the weekends or late afternoons do cars arrive and hangar doors start to open. Then, for a few exciting hours, the place is buzzing! Ultralights, experimentals, and spamcans jockey for space on the runway and the air is full of the sound of Rotaxes and four-bangers. It's

Like the well-trained wife she is, she sprang into action.

great!! If the weather doesn't cooperate, then the time is spent hangar flying, with weenie roasts, barbecues, and annual parties. On rainy afternoons, it is very soothing to sit in the hangar beside your pride and joy and listen to the roar of the rain on the tin roof and dream of perfect takeoffs, sensuous approaches, and "greaser" landings. Private pilots don't have your normal run-of-the-mill daydreams.

Small grassroots airports are becoming scarce in the country today and it's too bad. That's where general aviation began and flourished in the thirties. That's where the experimental and ultralight movements started.

I might digress here for a moment and explain three aircraft types to you: Ultralight, Experimental and Spamcan.

An ultralight aircraft is an *unlicensed* aircraft that must weigh less than 254 pounds, have a top speed of no more than 62 mph, stall at no more than 27 mph, and carry no more than five gallons of gas. It can tote only one person: the pilot. The lure of ultralights is that you don't have to have a pilot's license to fly one. Ultralights are also much more economical to operate than a spamcan. You are very limited as to where you can fly them, though. Many pilots who have lost their medical certificate for a non-critical reason can still fly ultralights.

Experimental aircraft are usually homebuilt planes that have been inspected and licensed by the FAA. There are no limits on speed, weight, fuel tank capacity or number of passengers allowed. An experimental must be flown by a licensed pilot and must be inspected by an authorized inspector every year. Many experimentals are only "heavy" ultralights whose builders decided to license the plane so they could build it stronger and add more refinements than the weight limits for ultralights would allow.

"Spamcan" is a slang nickname for any certified production aircraft. It's a kind of class snobbery practiced by ultralight and experimental pilots.

Whatever you fly, you can have a lot more fun at a small, private strip that caters to the pilot on a budget. To us, flying is something like a religious experience. We do as much of our own light maintenance as we can legally perform, getting it signed off by the resident A & P. When it's a really big job like pulling an engine or something requiring a lot of brute strength and ignorance, it's like an old fashioned barn-raising with everyone pitching in and helping. The wives bring covered dishes, the gas grills are fired up, and burgers and dogs are cooked. While the laughter and cursing from the planes echo around the rear of the hangar, the wives sit out front and chat, nap, or trade dirty jokes.

During annual time, you can see those pilots and owners out there, sweating bullets in the dusty, steamy T-hangars, covered with oil and grease, cheerfully swearing and bleeding as they pull fairings, inspection ports, heat muffs, seats, carpeting and interior parts from their planes. They grease the wheel bearings, swab out the bare interior of the cabin, wipe down the control cables with oily rags, and vacuum out the bits and pieces of grass, dirt and gravel that accumulate over the year.

I was lucky that, for a while, I had a small daughter. (Now she could beat me up.) By promising her everything on the menu at McDonalds, I was able to get her to crawl all the way back in the Tweety Bird's fuselage and scrub the inside with soap and water.

Once everything on your plane is open, cleaned and oiled, the resident IA (Inspection Authorization person) arrives. After a close look at the logbooks checking that all the important ADs are signed off, the inspector pokes, prods and climbs over the plane, peeking into holes and looking at every nut, bolt, rivet, and screw. The nervous owner follows him around, hoping against hope that he won't hear the dreaded, "Uh-oh!" from the inspector. Depending on the inflection, the "Uh-oh" could cost from $10 to $1,000. Annual time is always a trying occurrence. It helps, usually, to have some other owners like yourself to help you emotionally over this hurdle.

It's easy, particularly if you have the money, to just fly your plane to the nearest airport with an FBO and let them do the annual inspection. That can cost you $500 or more for a small plane, just for the inspection and paperwork; any needed repairs are extra. Your alternative is to do what the poor folk do—perform all the manual work yourself: the removing, cleaning, greasing, wiping down and any other chores your resident inspector wants you to do and then, after the inspection, put everything back together again. I have finally come to think like my dad. If your butt is going to be flying in the plane, you are going to be just a little more particular about how things are done.

I've gone plane hunting with some guys who have the mistaken notion that I know something about airplanes. Since I love to nose around at different airports, I always go and pretend I know what to look for. I have seen some very interesting examples too.

I have looked at some planes that were advertised as having "fresh annuals." I was convinced that if anyone had annualed those planes, they did it over the phone, long distance. There was rust on the control cables. Twisted safety wire had dirt and grease in the grooves and you could tell it hadn't been touched in ages. I checked the heads of the screws that cover inspection ports and fairings. If they were filled with caked grease and dirt, you could be sure that they hadn't been disturbed for some time. There would be jagged ends of safety wire sticking out in places just waiting to lacerate some poor slob's fingers. In one "fresh annualed" plane, there were cobwebs in the engine compartment.

Those shopping experiences make me glad that I do my annuals the way I have been taught to. I strip the plane, clean and wash everything I can reach and perform all the preventive maintenance I am allowed to do. After that is done, I call out my old man and he goes over the plane. After he has made me do everything again, I call the IA who does my inspections. I chose a guy in Kansas City with the reputation for being very thorough and nit-picky. I follow him around and watch everything he does.

I want to know if anything is wrong with my plane. The only time I really get nervous is when we do the compression check. Every year, I have given a big sigh of relief when all four cylinders checked out O.K. Top overhauls are expensive.

After the ordeal is over, I button my plane back up with the knowledge that her inside is probably cleaner than it was when she left the factory. Everything that could be checked has been checked and by me. Nothing was skipped and nothing was allowed to slide by with an "Aw... It's good enough for another year." In my experience, it's usually cheaper to fix it now rather than let it get worse.

"Frontier 503, Where-in-the-Hell Are You Going?!"

Why are they all laughing?

TRACON stands for Terminal Radar Approach Control. The TRACON room is where the air traffic controllers direct arrivals and departures at large airports. The inside of a TRACON room looks like Dracula's cave. You expect to see bats hanging from the ceiling and to hear wolves howling in the distance. The only light comes from the eerie green glow the large radar screens project into the room. Dimly seen figures cluster in front of each screen. They are the approach controllers who direct the "heavy iron" (airliners) into the traffic pattern at Kansas City International Airport. There is an unceasing low mutter of conversation from each station as the busy controllers work the traffic. Nobody is bored.

Chip, the approach controller, looked at the radar screen and slapped the counter in front of him in frustration. He looked again, grunted something under his breath, sighed and keyed his mike, "Frontier 503, where-in-the-hell are you going?" he cried. A roar of laughter went up in the room behind him. He turned to the man sitting beside him and asked, "What did I do wrong? Why are they all laughing?"

Chip was talking to Dennis Guy, an area supervisor at Kansas City International Airport's control tower. Chip was a student in a summer career awareness class. The class is taught by working air traffic controllers from the tower and uses the Enhanced Target Generator as a teaching aid. It's like a $2 million video game—except it's no game. The students are given an intense three-day course in approach control to acquaint them with the career possibilities as air traffic controllers. The laughing crowd behind Chip was composed of other students and off-duty controllers who had come into the ETG room to watch him work his "problem."

Frontier 503 had been heading zero-two-zero degrees, and Chip had wanted him to turn to zero-one-zero, a simple little ten-degree left turn. But when Chip instructed him to turn *right* to zero-one-zero degrees, things went to pot in a hurry. That's the long way around—a 350-degree turn. Brian Evans, the Air Traffic Assistant acting as pilot on the ETG had snickered and entered the command on the ETG's controller keyboard. Chip had then sat and helplessly watched his perfect approach to runway one-niner self-destruct in front of his eyes as 503 headed off the screen.

* * *

I had been taking my school's model airplane club for tours of the control tower at KCI for fifteen years. In 1984, Dennis Guy asked me if I could recruit students for the career awareness class. We started out with five students in 1985. In 1990, the class had grown to 26 students and I had to turn others away. Several students have taken it every year it has been offered, and one graduate is now starting college majoring in the courses needed to ensure entry into the FAA's training facilities.

Dennis Guy is the chief instructor. He sits beside the students at the controller's screen and prompts, cajoles, and helps them from their early weak, tentative commands on the first day, to judging their reactions to simulated emergencies on the third day when they have their final problem. Brian Evans is the "pilot" over at the operator's console and controls the planes on the screen.

One student who was trying to get Frontier 132 to assume a downwind leg for runway one-niner was informed that there were parachute jumpers in front of the plane's projected course. Did he turn the plane? Nope! He just keyed his mike and said, "Ahhhh, Frontier 132, be advised you have parachute jumpers directly in front of you; ahhhh, be careful." Another student, when told by Denny Guy to

116

instruct a plane to "Descend and maintain 3000 feet," got all flustered, forgot the correct phraseology, and finally blurted, "TWA 137, drop to three." Another winner was the transmission, "Eastern 342, you're cleared for a one-way landing on runway one-niner."

The kids are so entertaining and enthusiastic about the class that off-duty controllers stick around after their shift and lurk in the back of the ETG room to watch the students work their problems. Some controllers take students into the lounge and discuss with them the mistakes they made. Others give up their days off to help teach the class. It's really touching to see a hard-bitten professional explaining his or her job to wide-eyed 12-year-olds. I've been a teacher for over two decades and I have never seen a better example of what a career education class should be like.

One thing Denny likes to do on the last day of the class is put *me* in front of the scope. The kids love it! He always gives me "Problem 28." After five years, I still don't know too much about Problem 28. I usually self-destruct and start to cry after five minutes. All I know is that when I try to talk to other controllers about Problem 28, they all gag, shudder, and change the subject.

Problem 28 starts out with four planes entering the screen from each entry gate, and about thirty seconds later, four more call in and so on and so on. They call it "maximum saturation." I call it the gut-buster.

Last year, during my turn in the barrel, I had about twenty planes scattered all over the screen. I was holding my own and feeling pretty good when a new blip, a "pop-up," appeared right in the middle of the screen. It was "Cessna 77212 requesting clearance through the inner circle of the TCA." When that happened, I almost bit the end off the boom mike. (Cessna 77212 is my Tweety Bird.)

I stuttered and stammered for a few seconds, trying to figure out what to do. For a brief moment, I actually thought about trying to direct this 90-mph spamcan through all the high-speed traffic in the TCA. Then reality raised its ugly head. There was no way I could do this.

Ah ha! They want me to act like a controller, I'll act like a controller. I keyed the mike. "Cessna 77212," I snarled, "Descend to two thousand, three hundred feet and *remain clear of the TCA.*" I got a hoot of laughter from the watching crowd when I did that.

If I'm doing too well on my problem and Denny really wants to ruin my day, he makes Brian give me a plane that plows right through the middle of the TCA with his radio and Mode C turned off. Talk about a thrill! That experience told me more than ever that unless you have business in a TCA, give them, and yourself, a break and keep out. Those guys already have a full plate.

You know, over the years it's entirely possible that I may have been heard saying some pretty mean things about controllers. When they have chewed me out—in a very friendly way, I might add—for not doing exactly what I was told to do, I might have had some unkind thoughts. But let me tell you, until you have sat in front of a radar screen and seen what those guys have to do, you haven't understood what pressure really is. When I was in the hot seat, I think my toenails were sweating!

If there's a terminal control facility in your area, give them a call and arrange to take a tour. You should really see what the other side of the fence looks like. The tower people will be glad to have you. Better yet, get your flying club, EAA chapter, or local AOPA members to go with you. The FAA wants to do this, and believe me, it will really open your eyes as to what goes on there.

Ramp Check Man

*It was like exploding a firecracker
in an anthill.*

I turned my new gift over and over in my shaking hands, staring at it with a mixture of incredulity and cunning. It was the answer to a practical joker's wildest dreams. Immediately, all kinds of nefarious plans started to gallop through my mind!

One of the things we did in the air traffic control class was award the students trophies and certificates of training. This year, there was a special surprise award. Steve Baker, one of the controllers who trained the students, reached in a large box and gave each student a hat. It wasn't just *any* hat. It was a dark military blue hat with three large golden letters printed on the front. The letters were "FAA". Did it ever look impressive! I would have killed for one of those hats. Then they called me up front and gave me one, too. Oh Boy!

I felt drunk with power. This was just great! I started to plan my assault on the poor unsuspecting individuals at the little airports I frequent.

That night, I carefully laid out my wearing apparel. I wanted to look real intimidating; I mean, we're talking serious bureaucracy here. My wardrobe was ready: dark pants, white shirt, thin black tie, dark glasses, black shoes, white socks, and of course, the *pièce de résistance:* The Hat. It lay on the bed like a sleeping cobra, exuding an aura of latent malevolence that was almost visible. Sharon watched me go through my preparations silently for as long as she could. I didn't tell her what I was planning. I wanted the anticipation to build. I whistled cheerfully as I schemed.

Finally she snapped. "What the devil are you doing?" she demanded. I told her about my plan and showed her the hat with pride. "You idiot," she gloomily predicted, "you'll never come back alive from this one." I ignored her. There's a spoilsport in every crowd.

I borrowed my daughter's car, which no one at the airport had ever seen, and loaded it with my supplies. I was ready. Sharon kissed me goodbye and watched me drive off. She thought she would never see me again.

I knew that if I was going to pull off a stunt like this, I had to choose the right time of day to make my move. I'd selected a balmy Saturday afternoon; the air was calm and I could be sure the action at the airport was going to be intense. On nice days at our little field, you can usually find at least seven ultralight pilots in the pattern honing their skills doing touch- and-goes. There would probably be three or four more generally doing what pilots like to do best — pleasure flying.

Instead of parking down near my hangar, I drove to the remote "Visitors" parking area. As usual, when a strange car pulls into the airport, everyone on the ground craned their necks to see who it was.

In many of our hangar flying bull sessions at the airport we had wondered what we would do if the FAA suddenly drove up and started snap inspections and weigh-ins of planes. We all knew that if a hard-nosed inspector showed up, he could — and would — find something in our logs or papers that was wrong.

I got out of the car wearing my dark glasses and FAA hat. The lowering sun reflected off the glistening golden letters like they were on fire. I reached in the car and pulled out the FAA equivalent of a pair of pearl-handled Colt 45s: a ball-point pen and a clipboard. Yes-sirree Bob, the transformation had been made. I was no longer a simple mortal man, burdened with his worries and faults. I was reincarnated as RAMP CHECK MAN, He Who Fears No One.

I walked around the rear of the car and started slowly walking toward the hangars. The watching throng finally saw the letters on my hat. It was like exploding a firecracker in an anthill.

The next two minutes were a classic study in how fast the human animal can react to imminent disaster. All I could hear were shouts of warning and slamming hangar doors. It took me about two minutes to saunter up to the row of hangars. In that time, two cars drove across a recently harvested, rutted bean field in a cloud of dust, making their own roads to the airport exit. Another gaggle of panicked individuals was observed stampeding into the six-foot-tall cornfield and disappearing from view just like the baseball team in Field of Dreams. This was working great. I started to swagger a little.

By the time I got to the hangars, not a creature was stirring, not even a hangar mouse. It was a ghost airport. Strutting along the silent row of sheet metal buildings, my only accompaniment the crunching gravel beneath my feet and the hum of insects in the fields, I could feel hidden eyes from the cornfield watching me with burning intensity. I strode up to a hangar where I knew some pilots were hiding and beat on the door.

"Open up," I growled in a deep, menacing voice. "FAA!" Silence reined supreme. I smothered a snicker.

"COME ON, OPEN UP!" I yelled, "I KNOW YOU'RE IN THERE!" I waited, giggling crazily inside. Oh boy, this was going even better than I had imagined in my wildest dreams.

A timid, tremulous voice finally came from the other side of the door. "Who's there?"

I couldn't maintain the façade any more. "GET OUT YOUR PAPERWORK, BECAUSE IT IS I, RAMP CHECK MAN, DEFENDER OF STUPID RULES AND MESSENGER OF DOOM." I laughed evilly.

An enraged scream came from the other side of the door. "IT'S STARKS! GET HIM, GUYS!" They started to feverishly unlock and unchain the door, accompanied by some of the most astounding cursing I have ever heard.

It seemed like a good time to leave. I started my retreat. By the time they had finally torn the door open, I had a good 50-yard lead and thought I was safe. I ran down the road, laughing like a loon, with the baying, slavering herd thundering along behind me in hot pursuit.

I almost made it to the car. I would have, too, except two guys jumped out of the corn and tackled me twenty feet from safety. They delayed me enough for the lynch mob to catch up and lay rude hands on my person. In the ensuing dusty, swearing, sweaty skirmish I damn

"Open up," I growled in a deep, menacing voice. "FAA!"

near lost my pants and the rain barrel was dumped over me. Verbal abuse like I had never heard was heaped on my head. I laughed through it all. They finally started to grin and laugh, too. (Thank God!)

Then, as is usual after a successful practical joke has been pulled, the victims began their own devious planning. Someone asked me what other airports I had visited while wearing the hat. When I told them they were my first victims, the scheming started. I had several offers of rather substantial amounts of money for the hat. I turned them all down but did allow certain selected individuals to check out the hat for visits to other places of interest.

The reign of terror that summer was short but intense. One good thing did result from this episode. Everyone at our airport was scared enough that the paperwork in their planes is now up to date and complete.

"CAW! CAW!"

Cornfield: 1—Airplane: 0

Noah's Ark International Airport had been in an uproar for a week. All the pilots who could attend were down there every night watching things develop and enjoying this rare form of entertainment. There was a new plane on the field. It was a rare type of homebuilt — an amphibian, as unique to the Midwest as a flock of penguins. I'd never seen an amphibian, except some old WWII reconstructions at Oshkosh.

I'd certainly never seen one like this: a neat little two-seater, powered by a big Lycoming engine mounted in a pylon/pod setup on top of the wing. It was a pusher configuration with two main gear and a tailwheel/rudder combination. The gleaming white boat- shaped hull with retractable gear was beautiful. The owner had bought it as a semi-basket case and had worked two years rebuilding it. He had spent a week trailering the different parts down to the airport and putting them all together.

We all stood around making encouraging sounds and offering to assist, a ready and willing labor pool just panting to help. This was fun. The owner wisely declined our offers unless he needed some brute strength and ignorance to lift wings, hold things or just hand him tools.

The plane was finally assembled. It was inspected by two different

A & P mechanics, an IA, and finally, the FAA inspector. It was pronounced ready for flight.

The big day arrived, one of those golden summer mornings characteristic of the Midwest. The dew glistened on the grass. Only the occasional bird call disturbed the low hum of the grasshoppers chomping merrily away in the cornfields surrounding the airport. The corn was "as high as a elephant's eye," too. It was a bumper year. The crop was so thick and tall that the runway looked like a narrow strip mowed out of a thick, vibrant, verdant forest. The air was dead calm and cool and gave no hint of the searing temperatures, gusty winds, and gut-wrenching turbulence that would build up around noon. The conditions couldn't have been better for a first flight.

The owner had asked a veteran pilot with about 2000 hours to do the honors for the test flight. We all helped push the plane out of the T-hangar and the test pilot did a meticulous 45-minute preflight. He checked everything!

Then he got in the cockpit and cranked up the engine. It was given a good warm-up and the mags were checked several times. The carburetor heat was pulled on to observe rpm drop. A few slow taxis were made up and down the ramp to check out the tailwheel steering. Then the pilot shut the engine down.

The cowling was pulled from the engine and the A & Ps clustered around it looking for oil leaks. Then they searched for anything loose or amiss. All safety wiring was examined and castle nuts were examined for cotter pins in place. The throttle and heat-box linkage were checked again. Everything was scrutinized in the engine compartment. The final consensus was that everything, engine-wise, was as ready as it could get. The ailerons were operated, one more time, to make sure they were moving in the correct manner. It seems that, at least once every year or so, you hear about someone augering a plane in with reversed ailerons.

The pilot started up the engine again and the plane slowly trundled out to the runway. The air was still dead calm and cool. Conditions were perfect.

He made three slow runs up and down the runway at different throttle settings, feeling out the plane's steering response. Then he turned her around at the end, did one final mag and carb heat check... and took off.

The plane rolled about 400 feet and lifted off sweetly into a fairly respectable climb-out. The engine was roaring lustily and she seemed to have plenty of power. After he got about 500 feet of altitude in a straight climb-out, the pilot put her into a gentle bank to the right and started his crosswind turn. We all stood as a group and rotated around to follow him in his flight. He completed a pattern around the field and made a fly-by down the runway at about 1000 feet AGL. Everything seemed okay.

We could almost feel what was going on in the cockpit as we saw him explore the flight envelope of the plane. Slow flight, straight-ahead approach and departure stalls, accelerated stalls — he did them all. As before, she seemed to perform swell. The stalls all appeared to be gentle and straightforward with no nasty tendencies. The consensus of opinion from the audience on the ground to the plane's owner was that he had a sweet-flying plane.

The test pilot completed his turn from base to final and set her up on a long straight-in approach for runway one-five. The approach end of the runway is about thirty feet from the edge of the cornfield. The eight-foot tall corn made it impossible to aim for the end of the runway so all of us who regularly flew there knew to aim for the first runway light as the "end" of the runway. We knew from experience to avoid an emergency landing in a cornfield.

A cornfield is probably the WORST type of crop you can choose to land in. The rock-hard ears of field corn will totally destroy any plane that dares to take them on. We had seen what happened to a Cessna 150 that had landed short a few years ago. The plane looked like a crew of angry giants had spent a few hours beating on it with sledge hammers. It was totaled.

Anyway, he was on about a 300-foot short final when he pulled the power all the way back. That sucker sank like a stone. He added power and at that moment the engine "burped." It only lasted a second or two but when the engine came back on with a roar he was already behind the power curve and too low to recover.

The plane dropped into the corn with a horrible, hollow-sounding "WHUMP" about 60 feet short of the runway, or in other words, about 30 feet into the corn. The corn was so tall that the plane sank out of sight.

THE FIELD EXPLODED!! Fourteen zillion panic-stricken

Fourteen zillion panic-stricken crows erupted in a thousand directions.

crows erupted in a thousand directions. It was as if a dense black cloud was spewing from the bowels of the earth.

"CAW! CAW! CAW!" It sounded like an enormous 1000-pound bird had suddenly started screaming. Some of the crows were flapping their wings so frenziedly as they made their aerial exit, they left loose feathers fluttering down in their wake. Others seemed to be leaving small thin vapor trails behind them. They were very upset.

About two seconds after the terrified horde of crows exited from the field, there was the roar of an outraged Lycoming engine. The plane's bow appeared, surging from out of the corn like the *African Queen* emerging from the reeds. It was truly a dramatic moment.

The plane came to rest drunkenly, leaning over on a battered wing at the end of the runway. The engine shuddered to a stop. The cockpit hatch flew open and the pilot shot out of the plane as if he had been catapulted from a spring-loaded seat. He started to dance around the plane, waving his arms and shouting.

We had learned from hard experience that you don't run down to a wreck. By the time you get there, you are too pooped to do anything but stand there gasping for air with your tongue hanging out. We all piled into the nearest pickup trucks and roared down to the crash site in a cloud of dust with blaring horns.

The pilot was unhurt. As we thundered up and spilled out of the pickups he was screaming, "TWO THOUSAND HOURS... TWO THOUSAND HOURS... I'VE NEVER EVEN SCRATCHED A PLANE... TWO THOUSAND HOURS... NOW LOOK AT THIS MESS!!... BLEEP, BLEEP, BLEEP, DOUBLE-BLEEP... " his voice trailed off.

It was a mess! The main gear legs had been torn right out of the fuselage. When the gear went, it took the wing struts with it. Then when the wing struts went, the wings bent back and butchered the rear of the fuselage. And you should see what a cornfield does to a fabric-covered airplane!

The next two hours involved lifting the plane onto a flatbed trailer, towing it back to the hangar and beginning the discouraging job of taking her apart so the rebuild could begin anew.

Surprisingly, the owner wasn't really that disheartened. Now that he knew what a sweet flyer she was, he was anxious to get her fixed so he could fly her the next time. Besides that, he had already started complaining, while the plane was taking her test flight, that he didn't have a project to work on anymore.

The post-crash analysis went on for months. The final judgment from the "Official Noah's Ark What-In-Hell-Do-You-Think-Happened" jury was: BAD LUCK! Sometimes it happens.

III

The Dawn Patrol Flies Again

The Homebuilding Bug Bites

Warbirds for two.

"Ladies and gentlemen," the announcer said. "Would you please direct your attention to the south end of the field!" Two hundred thousand heads swiveled as one and all eyes searched the clear blue expanse of sky. 'Way off on the horizon I could see a cloud of little black dots hanging in the air.

The temperature and humidity on the flight line at Oshkosh had to be 100 degrees each. The fitful wind threw dust in my eyes and clogged my nose. I could feel a red tide of vicious, bloodthirsty Wisconsin chiggers inching slowly up my legs. My parched tongue was lolling out the corner of my mouth. I had been standing in the dust and heat for an hour, just waiting for this moment. Yep, just me and 200,000 other aviation nuts.

* * *

"Oshkosh" is actually a shorthand way of referring to the annual Experimental Aircraft Association Fly-in Convention. The EAA was founded in January, 1953 by Paul Poberezny and his wife, Audrey. They wanted to help preserve our aviation heritage and at the same time promote interest in homebuilding. Membership in the fledgling organization expanded as fast at the national debt. The first fly-in was held in September of that same year at Curtiss-Wright field in Milwaukee. The movement hasn't looked back since. The convention site was moved twice to accommodate the ever-growing hordes of enthusiasts — first to Rockford, Illinois, and then to the present location at Wittman Field, Oshkosh, Wisconsin.

Through it all, the EAA has resolutely stayed with its initial premise: Make aviation accessible to all while maintaining the highest possible standards of safety and quality.

Local chapters have sprung up in cities all over the world. Their monthly meetings make it possible for homebuilders, aviation nuts, and antique aircraft restorers to get together and share their knowledge of their beloved avocation. The two magazines published by the EAA, *The Experimenter* and *Sport Aviation*, give aircraft manufacturers and parts suppliers a means to advertise and promote their products. Without the aid, encouragement, and support offered by the EAA, many homebuilt projects wouldn't get past the gleam-in-the-eye stage.

The EAA can also put builders in touch with "technical counselors" to help with projects. In towns with no FAA Flight Standards District Office, this can be an invaluable aid in building your plane.

The EAA is very active in Washington, D.C. and monitors all proposed legislation affecting aviation.

So do I think you should join the EAA if you are a pilot, restorer, homebuilder, or anything else associated with aviation? YOU BETCHA!! I would wager there is an EAA chapter right in your own town. You can contact the EAA at P.O. Box 3086, Oshkosh, WI 54903.

At the convention, which takes place around the first week of August, you will see a cross-section of humanity and aircraft that is mind-boggling. Millionaire playboys with their own personal $500,000 WWII bombers rub shoulders with school teachers trying to build a $3000 ultralight for even less. Only at Oshkosh can you see a 1930s Ford Tri-motor parked by the supersonic Concorde, or a WWI Nieuport in the company of a stealth fighter. Oshkosh is a living history lesson in aviation.

The newest kits and completed aircraft are on display. Many planes can be built from scratch, following plans. But since this can be a pretty intimidating project, most builders will elect to build from a kit where the materials for the plane are delivered to your house.

Sometimes, even this pile of parts stacked in the garage can be too much for the aspiring builder. There is one last option.

The FAA stipulates that the builder of the aircraft must construct at least 51% of the aircraft. To that end, many kit manufacturers are offering what are euphemistically called "quick build" options, consisting of partially built aircraft that are up to 49 percent complete. It's a very convenient way to save a lot of work.

If you are interested in aviation and would like to investigate building your own plane, membership in the EAA is a must and a trip to Oshkosh to see flying examples of your dream plane is another must.

* * *

It was Warbird Sunday at Oshkosh — that one special day when the airshow is dedicated to the aircraft that, over the years, have fought for the sky. Pilots call it "Heavy Iron Sunday." I think it's one of the most moving events I have ever attended.

The little cloud of dots near the horizon grew closer. The massive crowd on the flight line grew quieter. Then you could hear it: a low thrumming drone. The crowd grew more quiet. The drone grew to a rumble. The dots became identifiable as a large flight of more than fifty AT-6 WWII trainers. The rumble became a roar and the exquisite formation passed overhead. The ground was shaking! Dust was falling off the grass. I stood there holding my breath, my heart pounding. What a moment!

Then the heavy bombers made their appearance. First a B-24 Liberator, then a B-17 Flying Fortress, and a B-29 Superfortress passed by in formation. The fighters were next, with P-51 Mustangs, Corsairs, Hellcats, Wildcats, and others not so well known, flying by in a cacophony of sound that left everyone slightly deafened.

The final act of the Warbird Sunday airshow is the missing man formation. It always gets to me. This time, it was something very special: a finger-four flight of Grumman "Cats." (Grumman Aircraft has been a noted producer of American fighting aircraft for over 50 years. The Wildcat, Hellcat, and Tigercat were all used in WWII. The F-14 Tomcat is one of our modern-day, top-of-the-line fighters.) The four cats started their pass down the field. Halfway down the runway, the Tomcat lit off his afterburners and pulled straight up into the blue.

As he accelerated out of sight, straight up, the public address system started to play "Taps." I stood there, my eyes glued to the planes and tears dripping off my cheeks.

The flight passed down the line and disappeared to the north. I looked furtively around and saw a lot of other people wiping their eyes and looking kind of sheepish – and proud, too. I know of some guys who get short of breath when they see a P-51 Mustang streak by with the Merlin engine giving out its distinctive wail. Other wistful macho pilots would happily part with a significant portion of their reproductive anatomy to get to fly a F-4U Corsair, B-17 Flying Fortress, ME 109, Spitfire, P-40 War Hawk, or P-38 Lightning.

Heck, I'd like to be able to just *sit* in one of those wonderful, historic machines for a little while. I used to go to air shows just so I could hear them roar by, look at them at their ease on the ground, and *smell* them after they had flown. The aroma of hot steel, high octane spirits, and oil is unforgettable.

I think that every sport and recreational pilot (and quite a few professional pilots, too) secretly yearns to own a plane that has a little romantic military history behind it – a warbird. The very word "warbird" makes you think of the "Knights of the Air" – Bishop, Rickenbacker, Luke, Richthofen, Nungesser, Immelmann, Guynemer and all the rest – names that will live in aviation history forever.

Unfortunately, for a lot of us who fly, the fuel needed just to run a mag check on some of those gas guzzlers would consume a whole year's flying budget. It is a well known fact that the ownership, maintenance, and flying of a WWII warbird is an enormous financial and logistic undertaking, not to be pursued by the fainthearted or anyone at all inclined to ask "How much do it cost?"

An alternate solution to the problem of warbird ownership is the construction of a homebuilt replica warbird, but some of them still take a fair amount of money, keeping them out of the reach of the average Joe. Also, the skill level needed to build a number of them is too high for casual builders. The world needs a reasonably priced (not cheap, in the quality sense), easy-to-construct warbird replica for all us Walter Mittys to have and enjoy. It should be easy to fly and not a real handful for the low-time pilot.

For six years, I had devotedly traveled the dusty, convoluted air trails to Oshkosh in the Tweety Bird. My one overriding memory of Oshkosh during those years is walking, walking, walking, until my knees finally gave out. Standing in the lines at the food concession is a close second, as is the fantastic case of heartburn from one of their infamous Bermuda Burgers that I am addicted to. It's all memorable. Oshkosh is more a religious experience than a mere fly-in. Sitting for hours on the flight line, the wind blowing a dusty gale, lines at the port-a-potties 100 feet long, getting lost in the fly market, a sweaty human gridlock in the display hangars — what heavenly memories.

I wandered the darkened flight lines late at night and very early in the morning so I wouldn't have to share the view with anyone else. I slobbered and drooled, moaned and groaned, panted and lusted over sleek homebuilts, classics, warbirds, warbird replicas, second-generation ultralights, and antiques.

In 1984, after returning from my annual pilgrimage to "The Big O," I was going through my usual post-Oshkosh-I-ain't-got-no-money depression. As public school teachers, Sharon and I don't have the riches of Peru, and the kits that turned me on cost far too much to even consider. I put aside thoughts of my dream plane for yet another year.

School started and my flying urges once again had to take a back seat to teaching math to my gaggle of "collie pup" middle school students. During my planning and conference period, if I was caught up with papers, I usually went to the school library and read books about aviation. I was thumbing through one of the many flying magazines I had talked the librarian into subscribing to for my model airplane club members, when suddenly, my life changed forever.

It was as if a bolt of lightning had hit me on the top of my pointed little head. It was INSTANT LUST!!! A WWI Nieuport 11... seven-eighths scale... with the markings of the Lafayette Escadrille... and a *machine gun* on top... oh wow!!! And last, but definitely not least, the article also said "Inexpensive to build!" Holy Biplane, Batman!!!

My heart began to pound like an out-of-balance VW engine. My blood surged in my veins, my myopic eyes misted over, the Walter Mitty lurking deep inside me pulled a leather helmet on and leaped into the cockpit with teeth bared. I was hooked.

I sent in $5 for the informational brochure about the Nieuport. It came, saying: she is beautiful; you don't need a lot of special tools to build her; it is easy to fly (they all say that); I could afford it. (Well, almost.)

I was convinced. I had to have one. My own WWI fighter! Three

It was INSTANT LUST!!!

days of sighing around the house got Sweetums to give in. Now, all I had to do was convince Tom that he wanted to build a Nieuport 11, too.

I needed Tom for a very special reason: he's an A & P and knows planes. He is also a whiz-bang, knock-em-down, drag-em-out, super-duper machinist. If he can't make it on his lathe, you don't need it! He can make, break, and then fix anything. Me, I use a hammer to put in screws. When I have to do some fine calibration, I just reach for a bigger hammer. My basic philosophy is, "If it don't fit, force it!" There was no way I was going to be able to build this plane without him.

Getting him interested in building the Nieuport was my next move. This had to be done very carefully. I had to make it look like it was his idea. No sweat. I've done it countless times before. (Tom lives only 15 minutes away from me – and our wives wish it were 15,000 miles.) I can be as subtle as a creeping glacier.

I needed the perfect bait and I already knew from experience what it was: I went out and bought a case of his favorite beer. (He likes some stuff that costs 99 cents a six-pack; you can either drink it or use it to strip paint.) I put the beer on ice, wiped the drool off the brochure, and got out my video tape of *Wings*, the 1927 WWI flying classic. I called Tom up and asked him if he would like to come over and watch a neat flying movie. He said yes, and I WAS READY!!! The web was spun and the spider was lurking ready to strike.

It was no contest. I don't think Tom (or his wife, Carol) will ever forgive me for having him over for the "movie." (She still doesn't know about the beer.) Tom's then-current homebuilding project, a KR-2,* went on semi-permanent hold and "The Dawn Patrol" was born. We ordered two sets of plans.

* * *

While we were waiting for the plans to arrive, I started to do a little research on the planes of WWI, and particularly the aircraft and men who flew with the Lafayette Escadrille. It was fascinating reading.

---

* Tom's KR-2 is a *really* little retractable-gear, low-wing, two-place show-stopper. It has a VW engine just like the Nieuports, but goes about three times as fast – 140 to 160 mph.

Sharon and I spent three days burrowing in the stacks at the University of Missouri's library in Kansas City and found that a number of articles were written about the Lafayette Escadrille in 1917 and 1918 magazines. The big surprise was that the library still had most of the magazines on the shelves. The research was fun. (The strange looks we got from the librarians when we explained to them why we wanted the material were great: "You're building a *what?*")

One very interesting book was a 1919 edition of *The Lafayette Escadrille* by James Norman Hall, a member of the original Escadrille. He is better known as the author of *Mutiny on the Bounty*. The book was mesmerizing reading and gave a valuable insight into the adversities that faced a WWI Allied pilot.

Let me pass on a little of the background of the planes used in World War One. They were significant in aviation, military, and American history. They didn't have a lot of horsepower and were basically a "light" aircraft by today's standards. Most were simply fabric-covered frames attached to an engine. Much of the danger associated with flying these early canvas falcons was caused by the poor quality materials used in aircraft construction at that time.

Another thing that made flying exciting in those days was the rather disconcerting habits that rotary engines had of either catching fire in the air or slinging cylinders through the cowlings. The rotary engine crankcase was bolted to the prop and the crankshaft was bolted to the firewall. The whole cylinder/prop combination spun at the same time and the torque was unbelievable. The TBO (Time Between Overhauls) of a Le Rhone 80 horsepower engine was 25 hours. Few engines reached their TBO because of an alarming tendency to fail at any time, at any altitude and under any power setting.

Include the fact that the rotary engines were two-cycle and used castor oil for lubrication, and you add acute nausea to the list of problems the pilots faced in those days. It only took about a one-hour flight behind one of those spitting, spinning, parts-shedding, noxious-smelling, noisy horrors to make you want to throw up everything except your toenails. Some pilots never did get used to it and were always sick while they flew.

One of the biggest drawbacks to flying a WWI warbird was the trickiness and sensitivity of the aircraft themselves. Some of them had their own legend (or curse) that followed them around.

Here are some examples: the Spad had a glide angle like a thrown rock; the Nieuport 28 shed fabric from the top wing in a dive; the Fokker Triplane was reputed to be a terror on the ground because of the itty bitty rudder; the DH-4, with its huge pressurized fuel tank between the pilot and observer, was called the "flaming coffin" by the unfortunate individuals who had to fly this ungainly horror in combat. If you crashed in an FE-2b, the pusher engine came smashing through the cockpit and crushed the pilot and observer. Some pilots called the F.E.8 the "spinning incinerator" because the rotary engine was mounted under the top wing which held the gas tank. When the rapidly spinning engine shed parts, as it often did, the red-hot shards of metal usually ruptured the tank.

The Sopwith Camel, considered by many to be the best Allied fighter in the war, was feared by the pilots from both sides. One week after the first RFC (Royal Flying Corps) squadron of Camels appeared on the front, it was the nightmare of friend and foe alike. It possessed unbelievable torque generated by its enormous spinning rotary nine-cylinder, 130 hp, Clerget 9B engine. Add this to the short-coupled fuselage and you had a plane that could dance through the air in the hands of an experienced pilot. A rookie flyer, on the other hand, was usually overwhelmed by this brute and many were killed by the Camel while trying their first solo flight.

All WWI planes burned like torches. Some pilots were so afraid of burning to death in their planes that they took along revolvers to end their agony quickly if they were caught in a searing inferno.

The Allied pilots were not allowed to carry chutes, even though they were available, because it was thought that this would "lessen their aggressive spirit." The German pilots carried and used parachutes and many German pilots were saved to fight another day.

All these facts made it certain that very few Allied pilots were bored while flying the early warbirds.

An Allied fighter pilot at the front in those days enjoyed an average life span of three weeks, or about 13 flight hours. So many of these boys were killed that fledgling pilots with as little as 10 hours of total flight time were sent into combat against experienced German aces. They were slaughtered.

Despite all these sobering facts, there was a waiting list of applicants to get into flying school and then on to the squadrons. Of all these early aviators, the fighter pilot was the hero of the hour. Those who were successful in combat, and survived, were courted by kings, queens, generals, and high society, and had countless beautiful, voluptuous women scratching and clawing to see if they could help, in some little way, to take the pilot's mind off the war for awhile. No wonder these men would do anything to escape the stench and squalor of the trenches, even if it meant almost certain death in the air.

There is no denying the aura of chivalry associated with combat flying during this period of history. Some examples of this were the victorious pilot saluting the rookie who was out of ammunition and letting him go out of the spirit of fair play; the vanquished pilot being lavishly entertained by the conquering squadron, or *staffel*, before being sent to POW camp; the elaborate funerals given a fallen ace by his enemies. All of these legends did a lot to disguise the horror of war and spread the legend of "The Knights of the Air."

In April of 1916, Western Europe was in the second year of war, and at the time, there was no method of synchronizing the firing of a plane's machine gun to the rotation of its prop blades in order to fire safely through the arc. During that spring, Roland Garros, a French ace, attached pieces of steel to the prop blades of his Morane Saulner model L monoplane and shot several Germans down using this very dangerous system; unfortunately, so many bullets ricocheted off the plates that he was as much a danger to his squadron mates as he was to the Germans. He finally shot his prop blades off and the prevailing winds forced him to glide to a landing behind German lines.

He was captured by German soldiers, who kept him from burning his plane. The German High command had it shipped to the factory of Anthony Fokker, the brilliant Dutch airplane designer, and one day later he had designed a system that enabled an aircraft machine gun to fire through the propeller and not shoot off the whirling blades. It was probably the most important contribution to military aviation in the war. The modification was quickly added to several Fokker E-IIIs and they were rushed to the front, where they spread terror through the Allied squadrons that came up against them.

The E-III became so deadly in combat that Allied pilots going up to fight against it began calling themselves "Fokker Fodder." The Allied high command frantically began searching for a plane to counter the E-III. One of the most memorable French designs to come forth at this time was the delightful, nimble little Nieuport 11.

The Nieuport 11 was nicknamed the Bebé (Baby) because of its small size in comparison with the other planes of that period. The Nieuport could out-climb, out-turn, and out-fight many of the German planes and could hand the Fokker E-III its lunch on a platter. When the Nieuport 11 was introduced into combat in the spring of 1916, it effectively ended the Fokker scourge, and the tide of battle shifted to the Allies' favor for awhile.

The Lewis .303 machine gun mounted on the upper wing of the Nieuport 11 fired over the top of the propeller arc and was a short-term solution to the synchronization problem. One major drawback of this arrangement was that when the pilot had exhausted his magazine's supply of 47 rounds of ammunition, he had to stand up in the cockpit, hold the stick with his knees, reach up — fighting the slipstream — and yank that 13-pound magazine off the machine gun and replace it with another one. All this frantic activity had to be done in the middle of a swirling dogfight. The Nieuport 11 was soon replaced with the more powerful Nieuport 17, which did have a synchronized Vickers machine gun firing through the prop.

Nonetheless, the Nieuport 11 was a significant aircraft in American military aviation history. It was the first airplane ever used in combat by American pilots flying as an "American" squadron. These pilots were the members of the famous French squadron called "Escadrille Lafayette." The squadron was formed in April, 1916 and was composed of American flyers who had volunteered to fight for France. Since the United States was neutral and did not enter the war until 1917, each volunteer had to join the French Foreign Legion to be able to retain his American citizenship. The original name given to the squadron was the Escadrille Americaine, but when German diplomats in Washington complained about neutrality violations, the squadron name was changed to Escadrille Lafayette in honor of the Marquis de Lafayette, who came over from France to fight for America in our War of Independence.

The American pilots were a wild and rowdy bunch. They kept two lion cubs named Whiskey and Soda as mascots. The lions were bought as cubs but soon attained full size. They were as tame as pussy cats and were taken into Paris on leave with the pilots, where they cut a wide swath at all the night spots.

Whiskey and Soda were very friendly and were allowed to run free on the airfield. Whiskey was the humorist of the two and liked to stalk up behind some poor unsuspecting soul, usually a stranger. When he was just behind his victim, Whiskey would emit a blood- curdling roar. The pilots would stand around when they saw Whiskey stalking someone and wait to see the hilarious action. This state of affairs lasted until Whiskey stalked a visiting French Inspector General, roared, scared the stuffing out of him, knocked him down, slobbered all over him, and then ate his hat. After that episode, Whiskey and Soda watched the war from a cage.

The American pilots chose a screaming Sioux warrior's head as their squadron symbol. It was copied from a box of Remington ammunition used in the Lewis .303 machine guns. Back then, Remington was called The Savage Arms Company. Tom and I decided to copy that Indian head insignia on the side of our own planes when — if — we ever got them finished.

The more I read and researched, the more I was sure we were building the planes we wanted. These little beauties were really going to be neat! Not only were they WARBIRDS! (say that with a snarl), they were *romantic* warbirds.

The designer of our replica Nieuports, Graham Lee of Circa Reproductions, had built the prototype Nieuport 11 in four months. We figured we had plenty of time to have ours completed in time to go to Oshkosh '85 — we would have a whole six months.

Oh, what fools we mortals be!!!

The T.L.A.R. Method

Bamboozling—the forgotten art form.

Our plans arrived on January 3, 1985. Tom and I had talked a lot about building these things and had decided to restrain our basic primal urges to start hacking and slashing away. Instead, we spent the entire month of January reading about and discussing the project. Finally on February 3, we began construction. I took two cases of beer over to Tom's house and we started off by building a table. Boy, were we proud! The next night we built both rudders! IN ONE EVENING! TWO RUDDERS! This was going to be a blast!!!

By February 17, we had two rudders, four elevators, two stabilizers and four ailerons ready for cover. That's not too bad for two weeks of part-time work. Graham's plans were easy to follow, and his design— using tubing, gussets and aircraft quality "pull" rivets—is very light, strong and rigid. The problems cropped up when we decided to "improve" on the plans. That's when the cussing started.

Luckily, we had some extra expert help. Tom's dad, Ernie, started out in the wood and fabric shop working on Fokker Tri-motors for American Airways, which later became American Airlines. He retired as a TWA flight engineer on Convair 880s. My dad, Burke, began as a line boy at Curtiss-Steinberg field in St. Louis. While employed by Chicago and Southern Airlines in Memphis, he worked with Roland (Doc) Anderson in the development of the heated pitot tube and pressurized ignition harness. He retired from TWA as a powerplant engineer specializing on the constant speed drive in 727s and 747s. He still thinks the Velie Monocoupe was the best plane ever made. Both dads are A & Ps.

Since the Nieuports are kind of a mixture of the old and the new in aircraft construction, our dads acted as our quality control advisors. Both of our QC critics were watching over our shoulders every second and offering advice every other second. Most of the time we heeded the advice. On the occasions when we decided to ignore it, they would both stand back and smirk until whatever Tom and I were working on blew up in our faces. Then they would tactfully ask us to try their way. It usually worked. Tom's dad figured out a real neat and time-saving way to build some of the specialty gussets needed for the wings. My dad carved us a beautiful prop blank to use on our propeller carver.

After about three months, we had the fuselages sitting on their gear and the wings pretty well framed up and ready for their first trial mounting. Tom's basement was getting too crowded with his half-completed KR-2 and the two Nieuports, so the projects were moved outside to hang the wings and rig. It looked like an aircraft assembly line behind his house. We used to say to the skeptics who came by, "Hey, this ain't no shade tree operation!" Well... it sure was then. We spent a lot of time wiping tree sap and bird "sap" off the fuselages.

My garage was the Fabric Shop. I used one of many different types of covering options: the 7600 process from Blue River Aircraft in Harvard, Nebraska. We chose it for several reasons.

Number one, it's fairly inexpensive compared to other covering processes. Big point!

Number two, it's simple to use. A bigger point!!! The 7600 covering system uses some very "friendly" ingredients that are non-volatile and fairly trouble-free. A specially treated Dacron cloth, ceconite, serves as the covering. The cement for gluing the cloth to the aircraft framework, cement activator and 7601 filler coat make up the other ingredients. The cement and filler are water-based with no obnoxious odors, and tools are easy to clean up using water. Only the cement activator is acetone-based, and acetone, for cleaning up the tools, is a fairly inexpensive ingredient to buy at our local hardware store.

Number three, the super friendly people at Blue River will bend over backwards to help you in covering your project. They sure did go the extra mile helping Tom and me as we muddled our way through the covering process.

* * *

As those of you who have ever built a plane know, the further you progress on a project, the more visitors you get and the less work you get done. When we first started on the Nieuports, hardly anybody came over. As progress staggered on and more people spread the word, our number of visitors increased — and so did the variety. Most of them were simply interested in what we were doing. They wanted to see how we were doing it and see if they wanted to build one, too. Some just came by to slobber and drool. Those who made suggestions usually did it in a diplomatic manner. We enjoyed having that kind of visitor. Most of them rolled their sleeves up and jumped right in there with us.

But we had a few of the other kind of visitors, too. Our most infamous one was a guy who showed up one night when we were framing up the fuselages. We didn't know him from Adam. He just opened the basement door and barged in.

"Say," he snorted, "I hear you two boys are trying to build two planes at once. Haw! Haw! Haw!"

Since there were two fuselages sitting there on the floor of the basement in full view, we knew right away that we had a real sharp one this time. Also, what was this "boys" business? He was younger than we were.

We let him wander around while we kept on working. Tom was fishmouthing diagonal braces for the fuselages and I was riveting them in place as he finished. We were thrashing right along as usual. This guy just kept running off his mouth about everything we were doing. His remarks were not designed to encourage friendly responses. No matter what Tom or I did, he could do it better, neater, and faster with more precision. If he wasn't telling us his way of doing it, he was finding fault with how we were doing it. Now, you've got to bear in mind that this guy had never built a plane, was not building a plane at that time, and will probably never build a plane, but, by golly, he could sure tell us what we were doing wrong.

He went over to bother Tom at the lathe for a while, and I was snickering as I riveted while I eavesdropped on the one-sided conversation.

"You're off on that angle... Why'd you do it that way, for gosh sakes? That's not straight... Is that the best you are going to do that? You'd better measure that again... That sure doesn't fit very good... etc., etc."

He never stopped. Tom's neck was turning a dull red. Tom has a fuse about a mile long, and it usually takes a lot to get him agitated. This guy was doing a bang-up job; Tom was only about two minutes away from doing grievous bodily harm. I was holding my breath because I didn't think this clown realized how close he was getting to a severe beating about the head and shoulders. I've seen Tom when he finally loses it and it's an awe-inspiring sight. If the guy is bigger than he, Tom will climb up his frame and stand with his feet in the guy's pants pockets so he can talk face-to-face with him. I got close to them so I could jump in and save this guy's life. Big mistake!!

OH, HORRORS!! He turned away from Tom and came over to me. It was my turn!!

"Can't you pull those rivets any better? You elongated that hole... That sure is a dull bit... You measured that wrong... You really ought to sharpen that pencil... That's not flush... You told him the wrong angle... You boys need to get better tools... "

I was gritting my teeth so hard my fillings were getting loose. I glanced up once and saw Tom over at the lathe grinning like a skunk eating a green persimmon and knew he was enjoying my eyes going bloodshot as much as I had enjoyed watching his neck turn red. Then I got my chance.

"How are you boys making sure the rivets are in the center of the tube?" our guest asked in his know-it-all, obnoxious, supercilious, overbearing, patronizing manner. Think about that for a minute. Any hole in a tube is going to be in the middle of the tube.

What a dork!

I looked up with an innocent, little-boy look on my face and simply told him, "Why, I'm using the T.L.A.R. method of hole alignment, edgement and spacing." Then I went back to work... and waited... and waited. I knew I finally had him.

He stood there with his beady little piggy close-set eyes going back and forth between Tom and me. He was thinking so hard you could almost see the smoke coming out of his hairy ears. I drilled a few more

**Tom was only about two minutes away
from doing grievous bodily harm.**

holes and put in a few more rivets... and waited some more. The noose was in the trail... he stepped in it.

"Well," he blustered, "Would one of you hot dogs tell me what T.L.A.R. stands for?"

I turned to Tom, my eyes wide in disbelief. Tom was ready. "Hey, Tom," I hollered. "Can you believe this?? This peckerwood doesn't know what T.L.A.R. means."

I turned to our uninvited guest and scornfully snorted, "I thought you knew about airplanes."

Tom sauntered over to the jigging table and looked at our visitor like he had just crawled out from under a rock. "You're kidding," he scoffed. "I thought everybody who knows anything about airframe construction knew about T.L.A.R. The EAA developed it and the FAA has okayed it for use in amateur-built aircraft. Why, the FAA is even thinking of modifying the 43-13-1A manual to include a chapter on the use of T.L.A.R." He cast another withering glance at our "guest" and swaggered back to his lathe.

I drilled a few more holes and pulled a few more rivets. Tom fish-mouthed a few more tubes. It was very quiet. We waited. Mr. Know-It-All finally went over the falls.

"Okay, okay! What in the heck does T.L.A.R. stand for?"

Tom strolled over to me and we got the table between us and faced our guest. Tom can look real innocent when he wants to. He looked as pure as the driven snow as he faced this pest and said, "Why, it stands for That Looks About Right." We waited for about five seconds and then fell to the floor, rolling around and holding our sides, laughing.

Ten seconds later, the door slammed behind our departed visitor; he was never to return. He wasn't missed.

That visit was the exception, rather than the rule. Most of our guests were welcome helpers.

No more than a week later, another know-it-all guy showed up. We always do a little leg pulling with our visitors until they catch on to the fact that their legs are getting stretched. This guy never did, and he was a pilot with over 1000 hours. He asked what kind of engine we were going to put in. We told him a 90 hp. Le Rhone rotary. He said that sounded good. "What's your top speed going to be?" he asked. We said about 140 to 160 mph. He bought that, too. Empty weight? 700 lbs. Working machine gun??? Of course! Oxygen system, transponder,

Loran C, ILS... he took it all in like we were voices from the Burning Bush.

Then he asked the clincher (are you ready?)... "How are you guys making sure the rivets are in the middle of the tubes when you rivet them?" I looked over at Tom and wiggled my eyebrows.

"Why, we're using the T.L.A.R. method of hole alignment. You know, the one developed by the EAA."

This guy didn't even bat an eye. "Yeah," he said. "I read about that and you guys are doing it just right." Tom and I looked at each other and quietly went back to work. All that good B.S. wasted... rats! Oh, well... onward and upward.

The Learning Curve

"Okay, what'd you screw up?"

Tom and I work well together. We can brainstorm a problem in quick time — and believe me, we've had a lot of practice while building the planes. We decided to construct a variant of the Nieuport that Graham details in the plans. Since we were going to be hanging a VW engine on the plane and going experimental rather than ultralight, we decided to build the Nieuport 17 wing and use it instead of the 11 wing. The only difference is two more feet of span; the extra square feet of wing area would help to offset the effect of the heavier engine and more robust airframe. If we had known what we were getting into, we wouldn't have done it. We have found out that it takes longer to revise something than to just go ahead and design it yourself.

When we are working together and everything is going well, we sing, yell, gossip, guzzle beer, sneak up and play little practical jokes on each other.

But when one of us gets quiet, that's when something's gotten screwed up. Once, when we were working on the fuselages, I put a gusset in backwards. Tom was hacking and slashing away over at the lathe. I was standing there trying to figure out how to fix my boo-boo without Tom finding out what I'd done. I stayed quiet too long. Tom suddenly spoke up, "Okay, what'd you screw up?" I cringed and showed him; five minutes later it was fixed and we went merrily forward again into the unknown.

After about 15 minutes, I noticed how quiet it had become over at the lathe. I crept over behind Tom, using my famous Kung Fu, don't-wrinkle-the-paper walk, and peeked over his shoulder. He was muttering some of his favorite four-letter incantations and I knew I had guessed right; he'd fishmouthed the end of a tube 90 degrees off the fishmouth at the other end. He turned around and his face fell when he saw me standing there, grinning at him. There's no way you can fix that. You just stand there, cuss for a while, pop the top on a beer, throw the tube in your ever-growing scrap pile, and drive on. We ought to know — we've done it a thousand times.

The first time we were able to sit in a fuselage was a red-letter day. So was the time when we mounted the first lower wing. In fact, every time we finally completed something new, we gave a sigh of relief and immediately, like lemmings leaping to their doom, jumped into building something we had not the slightest idea of how to even start. The first fuselage took three weeks. The second, four days. The first wing took two weeks. The next three took one day each. The first set of main wing spars took two weeks. The second set, five hours!

The aileron control pushrods and bellcranks were the biggest challenge. The first set of aileron controls took three weeks to fabricate. We'd build a set, put them in place, hook up the cables, try them out, throw them in the trash, cuss, and start again. It took four different tries before we succeeded. The second set took only four hours. Those suckers were the biggest bugaboos we had hit so far. Most of the problem was our placing of the outboard compression struts on the 17 wing, as opposed to where the compression struts were placed on the 11 wing. We didn't realize that the fact that the aileron bellcranks would be facing in instead of out would cause three weeks of agony.

The push-pull control rod for our planes' ailerons must pass under a wing drag wire, over a flying wire, and be contoured to miss both the control cables going to the bellcrank. It is also a differential aileron. (Twenty-one degrees up and 9 degrees down. The story behind the making of those is a novel in itself.) Graham's ailerons for the 11 model don't have to do any of the things I talked about. Another lesson learned: DON'T MESS WITH THE PLANS! DO IT LIKE THE DESIGNER SAYS!!! However, we finally finished them.

We had a very extensive correspondence with Graham in the building of these little jewels. We are sure he thought he was working with two idiots. He lives up in Alberta, Canada, and we had been so desperate on three occasions that we called him and begged for enlightenment. The first two times he seemed kind of surprised that we called, because the solution to the problems were so simple a moron could have figured it out. (Need I say more?) The third time we called, he was as friendly and nice as usual, but we noticed he tried to speak in words of no more than two syllables.

* * *

We had finally realized there was no way the birds were going to be ready for Oshkosh, and the depression from that made us decide not to go. We would work on the planes and save a lot of money by not going... that's what we said. About a week before Oshkosh, I started walking around the house with that strained look around the eyes: nervous twitch... runny nose... snarling at the wife and kid... kicking the dog. You know... an addict without a fix and needing one.

Then I realized what it was: I was going to miss Oshkosh! After five years of the same annual aviation fix, I was going to be cut off — cold turkey. Tom was looking kind of peaked around the gills, too. We started to rationalize. If Graham just happened to show up with the Nieuport, a few hours of digging in the plane and a session with Graham could answer a lot of future questions. Then we got the signal we were waiting for: a call from Oshkosh on the first Saturday of the show. "Graham's here with the Nieuport, and he wants to see you two." That was all it took!! Tom and I leaped into the Tweety Bird Sunday morning and thrashed our way up there to see him.

We flew up IFRR (I Follow RailRoads). We call it our Atchison Topeka and Santa Fe route. It's really very easy to do. It's also a lot harder to get lost. (My VOR usually starts to work about the same time you can see the VOR shack in the middle of the field.) We get to see a lot of rural America and meet some delightful people at the little airports we plop into.

Our first planned stop was Ottumwa, Iowa, but we had a tailwind and were getting 130 mph ground speed. Now, I know that for some of you "high dollar" guys, 130 mph is staggering through the sky. Well, let me tell you, for those of us who normally cruise at 90 to 95, it was great!! (The previous year, coming back from Oshkosh, fighting a fierce headwind, I had looked down and watched a tractor on a dirt road pass me.) Anyway, Tom and I decided to overfly Ottumwa and go on to Dubuque. We got there after three hours.

We were both under a lot of pressure when we landed. We taxied to the ramp, jumped out, and raced to the magic room. While we were taking care of ourselves, the fast and friendly ramp crew at Dubuque fueled the Tweety Bird and had us all set up to go. We paid the gas bill and leaped into Tweety for our final leg to Oshkosh. I fired her up, checked the oil pressure, called the tower, got permission to taxi and shoved in the throttle. We promptly started to go in tight circles to the left. What a rotten time for a brake to lock up! I happened to glance up and saw the line crew in the office rolling around on the floor, holding their sides.

Just then, the tower called and said those fateful, embarrassing words... "Ahh... Cessna 77212... what are your intentions?"

I looked out my window and turned red. I hadn't noticed that the line crew had chocked my left wheel. We shut her down, removed the chock, bowed to the cheering crowd, and told the tower if they would let us go, we would never darken their door again. They snickered permission to take off and told us to come back soon. We sheepishly left.

Tom had never gone into Oshkosh's Wittman Field using the special VFR arrival technique before. He's always gone in "no radio" and says he will never go in like we did again.

Both arrival methods utilize procedures different from anywhere else in the entire civilized world. For that one wild week, Wittman Field is the busiest airport in the world. This situation calls for special rules and regulations.

"No radio" arrivals are usually reserved for planes with no radio (that makes sense) or aircraft too slow to maintain the minimum speed in the "radio equipped" pattern, 90 knots or 104 miles per hour. A "no radio" approach waiver must be applied for by mail from the Wittman Control Tower. They mail you directions describing what you have to do to get to Oshkosh without a radio.

A "no radio" approach goes like this (these are 1987 procedures): Fly up the east side of the airport following the railroad tracks. Watch out for warbird traffic over Lake Winnebago. When at a mid-field location directly east of the airport, turn towards the airport while

We promptly started to go in tight circles to the left.

madly waggling your wings to tell the controllers that a "no radio" plane is entering the traffic. Insert yourself in the traffic pattern, follow the plane in front of you, land, get off the runway, take a deep breath, taxi to the parking area, get out, kiss the ground and you're there. Hurrah! It sounds pretty hairy but it's not near as interesting as a radio approach.

A radio approach is easier or harder depending on your point of view. You can see the arrival procedures printed in the EAA magazines, *The Experimenter* or *Sport Aviation*, several months before the convention. It usually runs like this: All aircraft flying into Wittman will fly to Ripon, Wisconsin, a small town about 15 miles southwest of Oshkosh. Then you fly single file up the railroad tracks with about 50 or 60 other planes in sight, like beads on a string, to the town of Fisk. At Fisk a group of air traffic controllers, somewhere in a field by a camping trailer, will talk to you on the radio, "RED AND YELLOW 120, WAGGLE YOUR WINGS!" If you do the right thing, you are allowed to go on to Oshkosh. I might add that you are told to never, never, never talk back on the radio. You just do what they tell you to do.

Then you finally enter the airport traffic pattern with about 50 or 60 other planes, every pilot as bug-eyed as you are. Next, you switch to the control tower frequency. These fast-talking folks will tell you which runway to land on and where to land on the runway—threshold or mid-field. You land, get off the runway, taxi to the parking area, get out, kiss the ground and you're there! Hurrah again!

If all this sounds like a bad case of air traffic overkill, then you've never experienced an actual arrival at Oshkosh during "Feeding Time," the Thursday and Friday before the first weekend of the show. You've got to remember that it has been estimated that up to *twenty percent of the flyable aircraft in the United States* will attend Oshkosh— most of them during that first weekend! That's a heck of a mess of airplanes to come into one airport. It's amazing how smoothly it runs. All these planes with all these "amateur" pilots flying into the same airport at the same time... it staggers the imagination.

Anyhow, we entered the "bomber stream" over Ripon and got into line over the railroad tracks with the rest of the bees going to the hive. I was listening to the controller at Fisk. She sounded like a tobacco auctioneer on a busy day. We wiggled our wings when she told us to and were told to go on down the pike.

We had a Cherokee about 300 feet in front of us, a 172 another 300 feet off our right wing and a twin Piper something-or-other real close off our left wing. I was over the railroad tracks where I was supposed to be and I wasn't about to move. The turbulence from the Cherokee was intense and I was going from stop to stop with the ailerons to keep Tweety on an even keel. The 172 kept trying to crowd in line. The twin had everything hanging out but the passengers and was still having to S-turn to fly formation on me. Staring eyeballs and open mouths were all you could see of the people in the other planes in our "formation." Tom's knuckles were white on the handhold in front of him. He kept moaning, "I don't like this... I don't like this... "

I glanced over at him and said, "Fun, isn't it?" A sickly grin was his only reply. I told him to check the traffic behind us. He grabbed the little mirror I keep in the plane to check my usually non-functioning strobe and held it up to the skylight to look behind us.

He took a quick look, put the mirror down, and went back to staring straight ahead. I asked him what he had seen. He looked at me with haunted eyes and said, "Prop spinners and air intakes... just prop spinners and air intakes... how much further?" He didn't look behind again.

Next, we got into the real three-ring circus at Wittman. We had to go waaaaaaay out over Lake Winnebago on a long right downwind for 27. When the tower finally let us turn on final, we were four miles from the airport and could count 15 planes in front of us and gave up counting the ones coming the other way on their right downwinds. Just as we were on about a quarter-mile short final, someone in a Bellanca triple-tail cut us off. There was a Mooney landing at the VOR, the Bellanca landed on the numbers. We splattered on the approach end of the threshold. I made one of my basic squat-and-leave-it landings.

We parked the plane, hugged and kissed the ground, staked Tweety down, and went and found Graham lurking around the Nieuport. It was Sunday morning, 11:45 A.M.

The Nieuport was beautiful. We took four rolls of pictures of the little jewel and poked and prodded all over it. Graham had redesigned the tail skid and it looked real good. It was certainly a lot simpler than our modified tail skid. I asked how sturdy it was and he climbed up on top of the stabilizer and jumped up and down on the tail. It worked fine.

One walk around the plane was the equivalent of writing a hundred letters. We asked a thousand questions, kissed Graham and said our goodbyes. We made a low level, high speed pass through the EAA hangars and the fly market on our way to the north end of the field to the Blue River Aircraft Tent. An hour's blabbering with Bob and Jerry gave us a lot of inside information on the 7600 process. Bob showed me a real sharp way of using pinked edge tape around sharp corners that I swear is magic. Supper was gobbled at one of the tents and we started the long mile hike back south to our camp, stopping on the way to pop into the tent forum given by Frank Kingston Smith, whose book *Weekend Pilot* was the reason I finally took the plunge and bought a plane. It was refreshing to hear that some of the stunts I have pulled in flying and kept a deep, dark secret, hidden in the depths of my soul, had been done by someone else — very refreshing.

We finally hit the sack very late and left at 5:45 the next morning (Monday). It was an all-time record short stay at Oshkosh: 18 hours. We had to get back to work on the Dawn Patrol. Our visit with Graham had inspired us and made us anxious to finish.

By August 8, we were installing ribs on the top wing, working on the cowling mold, covering the bottom wings, and starting to think about the engine. The end was in sight.

Attack Goose

Every home needs one.

One evening, I visited a friend's house to look at his homebuilt project. He has an enormous basement. It's heated. He's got lights all over the place. The vast expanse of shiny concrete floor is sealed and dust free. His tools are all systematically arranged and outlined on an enormous peg-board wall. He has more expensive power tools than the TWA overhaul base. You could perform surgery on his workbench. He even has a paint booth, for Gods sake! It is nauseating. As far as I am concerned, he is missing out on all the fun of homebuilding. How can you have fun when you know where all your tools are and everything goes right?

For me, every day presents a new challenge. I have a small three-fourths car garage. In winter it's colder than the river Styx. The cracked dusty floor is so cluttered that I lose tools for weeks at a time. I had to crawl under the wings of the Nieuports to get to the other side. My "paint booth" is the back yard where birds and squirrels gather from miles around to wait in the trees for me to start painting. Then, by squadrons, they dive bomb and strafe my fresh painting efforts. Building a plane under these circumstances presents challenges unappreciated by my more organized homebuilder brethren.

As if this weren't enough, I have a special set of problems caused by a peculiar member of my very own household.

On TV one night, an ex-burglar was interviewed. He stated that when burgling a house, dogs of any breed or size didn't bother him in the least but one animal could make the blood freeze in his veins and send him into headlong retreat: a "watch" goose. An enraged gander doesn't know the meaning of the word *fear*. The only words he knows are ATTACK! and KILL!

I have two geese in my yard, Gus and Gertrude. Gus, the gander, is one mean mother, the guardian of the yard and LORD OF ALL HE SURVEYS. He takes his work seriously, too. He usually hides behind a bush and waits for the next victim to saunter into his yard. He loiters, like an all-white Fokker triplane hiding in the sun, until his prey passes the point of no return going to the front door. Then he stealthily starts his stalk. He'll finally strike from six o'clock low, hissing like a leaky radiator. While he is taking plugs out of you with his beak, he beats the stuffing out of you with his wings. They feel like two-by-fours beating you around the ankles.

Gus's greatest triumph was the day he cornered the UPS man who was delivering more airplane goodies. The guy deposited the boxes at the front door, turned around and froze. You'd freeze too if you were faced with an enraged 25-pound gander at a range of three feet. Gus chased that poor guy to a fenced-in corner of the yard and went into high gear. It was a sight to remember, the UPS man frantically beating Gus over the head with his clipboard while trying to climb over the fence backwards. Gus was hissing like an enraged thirty-foot python. His head was darting in and out like a striking cobra, taking chunks of uniform and meat with each grab. At the same time, he was beating the living daylights out of his futilely battling victim with his wings. I came running out the door to the rescue when I heard the poor guy screaming, "CALL THIS $ ^ %$#@*%$ ^ %$# MONSTER OFF!"

The expected lawsuit never developed. I think he was too ashamed to admit he was bested by a goose.

Anyway, one day I was painting fuselage sheeting for the sides of the Nieuports in my garage. I was setting the beautiful, shiny, glossy, mirror-like sheets of metal in the back yard to sit in the sun to dry. It was setting the stage for one of my more monumental disasters. I should have had the music from JAWS on the stereo. Gus was on the loose, bored, and looking for entertainment. That big fat feathered fool waddled around to the back yard while I was inside, painting the

His head was darting in and out like a striking cobra,
taking chunks of uniform and meat with each grab.

last piece of sheet metal. Having decided to test whether the paint had dried, he left beak marks all over every sheet. I came outside, bearing my last piece of perfect paint work and saw Gus finishing his last taste.

I was able to kick his feathered butt around the house twice before he turned on me. I'd forgotten over the winter what he was really like. Rodan destroying Tokyo couldn't hold a candle to him. I barely made the house.

One day later, I laboriously water-sanded the scratches out and painted the sides again. This time the ferocious feathered fighters were locked up in their house. I could hear Gus honking in rage and hammering on the door with his scarred, gnarled beak as I carried parts out to dry. Boy! Was he hacked! I laughed all afternoon.

The Perils of Paint

Due for disaster.

The next month and a half were sort of a dream. Nothing went wrong! No major problems, no big cost overruns. It got so good, we became paranoid. We quit singing... no more practical jokes... we quit drinking beer. (Now it was serious!) We just kept on going... building top wings, putting on filler coats, covering top wings, final fuselage work, rib-stitching, taping, gluing, etc., etc., etc.

All the time we were looking over our shoulders waiting for the Hammer of Thor to descend. We were waaaaaaay past due on bad luck. (There were a few minor little things like Tom punching holes in the wing when his screwdriver would slip off one of the rib-stitching screws. Those incidents were expected and not upsetting.) It all finally came due on September 28, at 2:46 P.M. It was massive, quick and unexpected.

We had the bottom wings all covered and filled, ready to paint. We had dug deep into our souls and bought a new high-dollar spray gun with more knobs on it than a 747 panel. It was the most complicated thing we had ever seen. It was guaranteed to "give that professional look to your painting needs." We read the directions. (That was a first!)

The weather that Saturday was pathetic. It had rained three inches the night before and the rain was still coming down. Tom's back yard

164

looked like the Everglades. We were pacing like caged tigers in the basement because we were ready to paint. (I don't think either of us ever believed we would get to that stage.) We have to paint outdoors because of the space limitations and, besides, Carol would have KILLED us if we had gotten overspray on her washer and dryer.

About two o'clock in the afternoon, the rain stopped... the sky grew brighter... the trees stopped dripping. We took a cautious look out the door. It looked good... Let's do it!!!

We were so anxious to paint, we just took two of Tom's "cheapie" back yard chairs and set them up so the leading edge of the wing rested on the arms of the chairs and the top of the wing rested on the back of the chairs.

We hooked up the compressor, checked the oil and water trap and adjusted the pressure regulator. We mixed the paint and checked the viscosity according to the written directions. Then we adjusted the knobs on the gun and started to spray. A first horizontal light coat was applied. It looked great. Then the vertical cross coat was applied... It looked even better. We were standing back in awe, admiring the beautiful finish and patting each other on the back.

Then the wing over-balanced on the back of the chair... did a beautiful three-fourths back somersault and landed wet side down in the mud, wet grass, bow-wow, meow, chirp-chirp, and all the other unmentionable things in the glutinous ooze. All the bad luck we had been accumulating for two months had fallen on us like a toad jumping on a June bug.

There was a stunned, unbelieving silence... we couldn't even find words to express ourselves (yet another first!). I looked over at Tom and he looked at me. He shrugged his shoulders; I started to cry. We picked the wing up and turned it over to look at all the variety of goodies stuck in the paint. It looked like a green and brown pizza with interesting little splashes of color scattered around to give it variety.

With tears running down our faces, we carried it into the house like we were carrying a Spartan on his shield after Thermopylae.

A few hours' work with foam brushes and reducer cleaned the wing and brushed out all the marks of battle. This was all done in a dead silence, punctuated by deep, heart-rending sighs.

Then Tom said, "You know, I like the way you react to things like that. You didn't get all excited and scream and shout."

It looked like a green and brown pizza.

I looked at him. "What else could I do?" I asked. "It had already happened. Besides, we were due."

He admitted the truth of that statement. There was a long pause. I looked at Tom; he looked at me. We shrugged and grabbed another wing, took it out and painted it. It came out great. We had used up our accumulated bad luck, survived, and were now working with a clean slate. A long, open road was ahead of us once again.

Then the weather turned sour. If it was nice, it was too windy and little unidentifiable things fell from the trees and marred the paint. We got so we would spray with our right hand and pick goodies with the left. If the wind didn't blow, it rained. Progress really started to slow down. A panic call to Blue River Aircraft Supply told us that the Flexi-Gloss paint we were using could be applied using a foam brush. We tried it. It looked as good as the sprayed finish (*our* sprayed finish). The painting was moved indoors. We staggered and thrashed our way onward into aviation history. The painting actually moved a lot faster, and besides, now we were being authentic in our finish. (At least that's what we were going to tell the skeptics.)

* * *

On the few occasions that my enthusiasm waned on the project, a quick early morning viewing of *Wings* started my blood flowing again. "There's a Gotha over Mervale... two thousand meters... go get him, boys!" Did you know that William Wellman, the director of *Wings*, was a member of Escadrille Number SPA-87 and flew Spads over the Western Front? (Clara Bow wasn't too bad, either. She could make a bishop kick in a stained glass window. Some of the beauty queen "actresses" of today seem like three-day-old boiled cabbage in comparison.)

On Saturday morning, October 13, things really started to happen. I was home in my unbelievably cluttered garage, rib-screwing the fabric on the next-to-last top wing half when the phone rang. It was Tom.

"Do you have any extra 1.8 ounce fabric?" he queried in a strained voice. I wondered at the question... something was wrong!

"Why do you need some fabric over there?" I asked, with fear in my voice. "All you're doing at your house is filling and painting." There was a long pause on the phone.

Then he muttered in a low voice, "How hard is it to patch holes using the 7600 process?" I then knew the worst.

"WHAT'D YOU DO?!?!?!?" I screamed. It was like pulling teeth, but after a few minutes I extracted the whole sordid story. He was getting ready to spray outdoors because our weather, for some insane reason, was good for a change. While he was carrying one of the lower wings outside, the storm door slammed shut... on the wing. It plunged the door handle right through the top of the wing. Tom said the sound was something he will never forget... like a tomato stake being driven through a plastic milk jug. The slit was six inches long and about an inch wide.

I asked him what he did when it happened. Apparently, incoherent hollering took up the first ten seconds. He spent the next thirty seconds looking for a kid or a dog to kick and couldn't find either. Cussing had to suffice. (Carol said he reached a career high in volume, ease of delivery, and enthusiasm. He danced around the back yard screaming, waving his arms and running in circles. He did this for about five minutes and never repeated himself. The neighbors came outside, and some were enviously taking notes. It was a virtuoso performance... a verbal tapestry of baroque profanity... truly a masterpiece. I'm sorry I missed it. I'm sure it is still lurking around in his back yard, a malevolent greenish-black cloud just waiting for an unwary victim to come within range.)

I quickly loaded up my rusty old 1971 van with fabric, glue, activator, pinking shears – and most important, cold beer – and headed over to Tom's.

When I arrived, he was still looking pale and distraught, so I put a frosty beer in each of his palsied hands and sat him in a chair in the shade so he could watch, guzzle, and recover his breath while I worked on the repair. It only took 45 minutes to make the patch, and, by stealing Carol's hair dryer to hurry the drying, I soon had it ready to paint. Tom's face had, by then, recovered its normal healthy color, and we soon were back on schedule and thrashing right along in a cloud of overspray, accompanied by the gentle pitter-patter of a shower of asphyxiated bugs.

That day, all the bottom wings, tail feathers, ailerons, and one top wing were spray painted with the silver gray base. They looked great!! Another frantic phone call had gone out to Harvard, Nebraska, and the Blue River boys had told us what we were doing wrong when we spray painted before, and this time the spray finish looked better than the brush. We hadn't been putting on enough paint. The brush finish still looked good enough for trim, and we went ahead and used it for the roundels and lettering.

The guys and gal of Blue River Aircraft Supply will really help you with your problems. These good people always seemed very interested in what we were doing. They really wanted the birds to look good. When I called up, I usually started out by saying, "Hello there, you handsome devil!!" or "you sweet thing," depending on who answered the phone.

I would then hear whoever answered the phone put their hand over the mouthpiece and yell, "IT'S HIM!" Then their other phones would get picked up because they all wanted to hear of The Dawn Patrol's latest exploit. I'm sure they have a mute button on their phones, because sometimes, when I told them of the latest of our trials and tribulations, there would be a long pause before someone answered. When they finally came back to the line, it sounded like they had just run a mile, and the sounds of unrestrained mirth could be heard echoing in the background. I think whoever was laughing the least got to answer our question(s). They really went the extra mile in helping us. Tom thinks they used us as an example of what two "turnip brains" could do wrong using Flexi-Gloss and adjusted their instructions after every one of our calls.

* * *

We had our registration numbers reserved with the FAA and were very lucky in getting what we wanted. It took a few long-distance calls to Oklahoma, but was worth the cost. I got some very helpful ladies in the records section who went through the numbers and helped me see what was available. I reserved N124DS for me and N124TG for Tom. The 124 was the original squadron number for the Lafayette Escadrille. I really wanted that. Sharon and I had spent many frustrating hours in the University's stacks trying to see any rhyme or reason in the rudder numbers we saw in the pictures. Graham finally told us they were the planes' manufacturer's serial numbers and had nothing to do with the squadron numbers. The N and S on the French squadrons' rudders stood for Nieuport and Spad.

Tom was working on the brakes, and after 32,654 revisions, they were almost ready to be built. Painting the roundels on the wings was my job. I resolved to do such a bang-up job on the roundels he would have trouble choosing the wings for his plane. If I'd only known what a joy they were going to be.

I hauled the wings over to my house and made my templates. There were four lower wing roundels to do and eight upper (top and bottom). That's twelve of those suckers. I started to feel uneasy... That's a lot of masking tape to apply. I wasn't at my best at that. Doing the Tweety Bird's decorations had driven a loathing of masking tape deep into my soul. I never got the knack of keeping the paint from creeping under the tape and leaving a ragged, unsightly line of scraggly color on the pristine undersurface. I got my supplies together, thought positive thoughts, and with slitted eyes and a sneer on my lips, strode into the garage with a wing, paint, tape and a prayer.

I painstakingly masked off a roundel on a lower wing and applied brush coats of the red and blue paint. They were the outer and inner colors of the French insignia. I paced around the wing, waiting for the paint to set up. It set up. I approached the tape... and very slowly pulled it off. It was terrible!! Little thready lines of red snaked their way over the beautiful shiny gray base. That did it! I started to yell using the usual four-letter lexicon I reserve for times when emotion overcomes me. As Mark Twain said, "When angry, count ten. When very angry, swear."

Just about then, Sharon opened the door into the garage, stuck her head in, and cheerfully chirped, "Having a good time, dear?" It was the final straw!

The resulting fiery blast of screamed obscenities blew the hair back from her ears and frizzed her eyebrows.

Trying to sleep on the couch that night, I reflected on the injustices of life. I had told her over and over that I wasn't yelling at her. Apologies had gushed from me like Old Faithful on a good day. It hadn't done any good. Once again, I had fouled the nest and been banished from my warm nuptial bed occupied by a passionate, fragrant, loving wife to the cold, short, lumpy couch in the living room occupied by a hot, loving, smelly hound dog. It wasn't an equitable trade-off. Ah, the mystery that is woman. I had already sneaked into the bedroom twice to try and reconcile myself with her but all my efforts were in vain. That lady was mad!

When I tried the second time to get back into bed with She-Who-Must-Be-Obeyed I had noticed that Bagherra, one of our cats, had mistaken the floor for a litter box and left a souvenir right in the middle of the hallway. In a bitter mood, I decided that it was not my problem and went back to sulk in my cold, chaste bed. Bad decision!

About an hour later, I heard Sharon get out of bed and pad across the floor of the bedroom. I thought she was going to go to the bathroom but when I heard her give a sudden gurgling gasp, I knew differently. The gasp was followed by an inchoate scream of inarticulate rage. I knew she'd turned down the hall and stepped right in the middle of the feline land mine. She was hopping around in the dark on one foot, bumping against the walls of the hallway, screaming words that would make a Marine D.I. envious.

It was then that I made my second major mistake of the night. Like a rookie guerrilla fighter on his first ambush, I lost my nerve and broke cover. I couldn't help it! I lost control: she heard me giggling on the couch. I don't remember much of what happened from then on.

I found out later, when I regained consciousness, that she had been coming out to forgive me and welcome me back into her bed for one of our wildly passionate, you're-forgiven make-up sessions. Needless to say, the rest of the night was strained in the Starks' household.

It took an expensive dinner out, flowers, and another night sleeping on the couch before I was back in her good graces. After that episode, when I was about to remove tape I'd yell, "OKAY, GIRLS, I'M GETTING READY TO DO IT!!" Sharon and Trish would then leave the house and huddle outside while rumbles, grumbles, sharp exclamations, and exhalations of green smoke would spurt out of the cracks and crevices in the garage.

I eventually found out the reason for my problem. Flexi-Gloss is a water-dispersible polyurethane paint. The water in it just goes right through regular masking tape. I got some 3M #471 blue fine line tape. Flexi-Gloss paint sticks to this type of tape and leaves a sharp, clean-cut shear line when pulled properly. That was used for the first mask. Then by using a good quality automotive crepe masking tape to stick the masking paper to the 3M tape, a sharp, fine line could be achieved without any bleed-under. Another hurdle cleared. The roundels were then a time-consuming but not unpleasant chore. I was so proud. Tom came over to check on me and I showed him the stacked wings with a flourish like an artist showing off his latest masterpiece. He was agreeably impressed.

I then had to go over to his house and see the brakes. I was very favorably impressed. We spent so much time congratulating each other and patting each other on the back, our wives got tired of the sickening display and went to a movie so they wouldn't have to hear it any more. That was okay with us. We could build, cuss, and guzzle beer to our hearts' content without the inhibiting female presence. Progress staggered on. That's what homebuilt planes are all about. Having fun. Building one is almost as much fun as flying one.

Contact!

The Dawn Patrol FLIES!

By November 28, the brakes were completed on Tom's plane and the patches that covered the cable exit slits in the tail feathers and fuselages of both planes were glued in place. After looking at leather, which was priced by the square inch, we decided to use marine vinyl seat cover material for the patches. It looks like leather and is water resistant. We also used it for the cockpit coaming over high density foam water pipe insulation. After it was laced in place, it made the planes look a thousand percent better. They were starting to look like *fighters*.

On January 5, we turned a big corner. We finished the fuselages from the firewall back—almost. The only things left were the side sheeting on the front (no big deal) and the Indian head insignias on the sides. Our wives, both amateur artists, were all set to do the insignias and had already cut out their stencils. I called up the folks at Blue River Aircraft and told them I needed a color I described as "Screaming Eagle Brown" for the Indian's face; they came through again with a color called Phoenix tan. The instrument panels were installed and were burnished like the cowling on the "Spirit." We had two cowling bowls pulled out of the super-duper mold that Tom had built. The brakes were installed and worked! Tom had outdone himself on them.

The last really big design hurdle we had was the steerable

tailwheel. First of all, we had to have one. Our field has a narrow runway with rough corn fields on one side and a deep, weed-filled ditch on the other. When someone ground loops, we either say "He cleaned out the ditch," or "He chopped a couple of bushels of corn." The pilot who test flew and then wrote the pilot report about the Nieuport had only one exciting experience, and that was due to the lack of a steerable tailwheel.

A homebuilder has three options: 1) a tail skid, 2) a free-castering tailwheel or 3) a steerable tailwheel.

All a tail skid does is drag along the ground behind the plane like a miniature plow. If you are taxiing on grass, it digs in pretty good and keeps you and the plane going where you probably want to go. However, if you are taxiing on a hard-surfaced runway, the tail skid just "skids" freely along the surface like a drop of water on a hot skillet. The plane can swap ends faster than a dog going after a flea on his tail. Tom and I weren't really interested in having that much variety in our flying.

A free-castering tailwheel swivels freely through 360 degrees, and with the short length of the Nieuport it had the potential of being even more exciting than the tail skid. We weren't too keen on doing that, either.

A steerable tailwheel is connected by cables to the rudder bar and would move in concert with the rudder. It *should* do the trick.

Tom and I spent about two sweaty nights and threw away a lot of "new" parts in our search for the right way to do it. Graham's idea of using a fiberglass rod as a shock absorber saved us a lot of grief and works extremely well. Our only problem was the mounting of the completed tailwheel assembly to the covered tail skid frame. The skid frame is covered to form a sort of ventral fin to keep the plane from "dog-tracking" in the air. We looked like two devoted acolytes in front of the altar of a primeval god as we sat crosslegged on either side of the tail, on the floor, with our heads resting on our hands and staring fixedly at the tail skid frame.

There would be a long silence and then Tom would mutter an idea. There would be another long silence and then I would mumble, "Okay. What happens when..." There'd be another long silence and then Tom would say, "How about we do this to counter what you said and then do this... mumble... mumble... mumble?" Looooong silence. Then

Tom would leap to his feet, yell "LET'S DO IT!!" and scramble over to the lathe while I would unlimber the tin snips and plug in the band saw. For about ten minutes there would be the sounds of furious activity and the smell of hot metal. Then we'd hunker down back at the altar again to try it on. The silence would end with a cloud of profanity when we finally realized why it wouldn't work. Next would be the sound of parts hitting the trash can and the whole scene would start all over again.

This went on for two days, and in the end we had one heck of a neat tailwheel setup. It really works great and is lightweight and simple. Science and Technology triumphed again.

On January 9, we started on the prop carver and got the major frame completed in just one night. I knew my little router was going to give up the ghost doing this, but we were committed. We are just too cheap when it comes to buying something when we know we can make it for about two or three times the same price. (It usually comes out that way.)

The next month and a half was boring. We had a lot of piddly little things to do like rudder stops, engine mounts, carve a trial prop, insignia, etc., etc., etc. The wives did a great job on the Indian heads, although it took two weeks to do them. (That really crimped Tom's and my style because they inhibited our freedom of expression in the basement.)

On March 5, we got our first engine crankcase assembled with the other right behind it, ready to assemble. All the other engine parts had been cleaned and inspected. Then, a strike that affected TWA (where Tom is a machinist) really brought things to a screeching halt. We did a lot of little things like seat belts and motor mounts, cowlings, machine guns, and final touch-up painting, but we were both having a severe cash flow problem: we didn't have any cash to flow. I mean the kitty was *flat* and we needed to buy instruments, engine controls, and a host of other goodies to finish the beasts.

* * *

Tom and I bring new meaning to the word "tight." The word "retail" makes us flinch. We became familiar faces at the local metal salvage yard. Their junk yard dog, Panzer (like the tank), got so he actually wagged his tail when he saw us.

We spent many happy hours digging through the teetering piles of sheet aluminum, channel stock, and plate. One package of Band-Aids was good for each visit. We figure we saved about 40% to 50% on our materials by hitting all the places in Kansas City that carried surplus material. We saved a lot of money, but we bought only the best.

By April 1, the end was definitely in sight. (Finally!!) The paperwork with the FAA was almost finished, and the planes looked completed. The burnished cowlings were done except for paint. Tanks were in and fuel systems were installed.

Three different heat box designs hit the trash can before I got what I wanted. Once again, the "cheaps" struck Tom and me. There was no way we were going to pay the prices demanded for ready-made heat boxes. Tom was working on the heads for the engines, so I landed the chore of designing the boxes. We finally ended up with a real neat little cube three inches on a side and fitting right on top of the carb with the air filter bolted directly to it. Neat, small, and fool-proof. Then the "cheaps" hit again when we were looking for throttle quadrants. You-know-who got the job of designing and building them, too. Tom was lapping valves, torqueing heads and other neat things, and he decided to get me out of his hair.

Once again, the R and D curse hit me. The first quadrant took three days (three different tries). The second, 45 minutes. Then we put them on, then we threw them out. We had to completely change the cable arrangement from push to pull to get the throttle articulation to work as smoothly as we wanted. This only took another evening, but time was getting short.

Tom's plane was rigged up in the back yard by May 4. During the rigging, the curse struck again. We were mounting the lower wings when, to our horror, we watched the root end of the leading edge press a big dent in the forward fuselage side sheeting.

The wings were pulled off and the head-scratching and cussing started. A quick skull session had me very carefully cutting the fabric away from around the root rib. By simply drilling out two rivets, pushing the leading edge end of the rib ¾" towards the tip along the leading edge tube, and placing two new rivets, the problem was solved. The little ¾" stub was cut off and the wings remounted. Time to do... 20 minutes.

We tweaked the flying and landing wires to Graham's specs and declared Tom's Nieuport ready to go, except for the patching of the root repair work. The wings were thrown into my truck and I raced home, dug out the 7600 glue, filler, activator, fabric, tape, and paint. In one afternoon, I was able to patch, shrink, tape, fill, and give two coats of paint to the new wing roots, and we were once again ready to roll. All this was done on a day when the humidity was 93 percent. That 7600 process can't be beat. I took the wings back to Tom's. We pushed his fuselage up to the garage and got it ready to permanently mount the engine.

We had also become very nervous about our deadline, which was rapidly running out. We knew that if we were going to be able to fly these sweeties to Oshkosh, we were going to have to have the whole 40 hours on the birds before the FAA would let us out of the airspace cage around our airport.* Sooooo, we ordered two props from Ed Sterba, a VW prop specialist who advertises in *Sport Aviation*. He seemed to get really interested in the planes. His prices are very reasonable, and he makes a beautiful prop.

The engines were finally mounted on May 18, and both planes were pushed out into Tom's front yard and tied to trees. We both offered up a prayer to Icarus and started the litany... "Switch off... Throttle closed... (five cranks)... Switch on... Throttle cracked... CONTACT!!!"... Nothing.

Again and again. Nothing. We checked spark plug wires. Then we switched them to the correct cylinders. Next we changed the lines from the fuel pump around so it would be filling the carburetor instead of sucking the gas out and got ready to try again. (By this time, both our dads were rolling around in the yard, holding their sides.) Tom was handling the throttle and I gave the prop a healthy flip. BRRRRRAAAAAAWWWWWWW!!! The throaty bellow of the mighty 1700 cc. Volkswagen engine split the air of sleepy Gladstone, Missouri, for the first time.

We let it idle and ran to the other plane. After first changing the spark plug wires and fuel lines around, we went through the starting

---

* The FAA requires that a new experimental aircraft fly its first 40 hours in a restricted flight area, usually a circle with a radius of 25 miles around the plane's home airport. If the plane is using a certified aircraft engine, the time can be lowered to 25 hours.

ritual. It started on the first flip. Both planes sat there like two sewing machines ticking over at 600 rpm. The sound was pure bliss.

I almost cried... I never thought we were going to get that far. We liked the sound so much we recorded 20 minutes of it and played it while we worked. (That should give you an idea of how weird we are.)

* * *

On May 20, we fell into a dream deal. We were really looking for an enclosed hangar to keep the little warbirds in, because they looked sooooo pretty that in a shade-hangar it would have been hard for a passerby to keep hands off. Enclosed hangars in Kansas City are either unavailable or only for the *rich*. Then Virgil called me and said he knew of a hangar for rent. The airport was an additional 30-minute drive from us, but the price was attractive.

So, on May 27, the Dawn Patrol was trucked to Mount Muncie International Airport at Lansing, Kansas for final assembly. (We almost caused several wrecks towing the fuselages down the turnpike to the airport. A car would drive past and then start to weave as the driver would turn and try for a second look. Even then, they looked neater than neat.) After three days of late-night work, both planes were assembled and ready for inspection and taxi tests.

I took our final logs, papers, and other goodies to the FAA to make arrangements for final inspections. That part was painless. One piece of advice: Let the FAA know what you are doing and check in with them several times with plans, pictures, logs, and completed parts to show them your workmanship. They can be very helpful when they know you are serious. I bet they get sick and tired of seeing some wild-eyed character come crashing through the door, waving a set of plans, and crying, "Ah'm agonna built me a hair-plane!!" Once they see you're for real, they can be very helpful and also tell you ahead of time if they don't like something you are doing.

Judging from some of the horror stories I have read concerning the FAA and homebuilt aircraft, Tom and I must have been really lucky in getting the gentleman who was assigned to our case: Arthur DeSalme, an old-time FAA inspector who was really interested in the planes. On my first visit to him, he spent an hour and a half going over the plans, pointing out several places where he wanted Tom and me to pay special attention to detail. This man was great! After we had finished the rudders, I took them up to show to him. He got so excited about them he showed them to everyone in the office. Then I took him some covered control surfaces. He liked them, too.

By Sunday, June 2, the Dawn Patrol was ready to start our taxi test program. What a thrill. Our little field is very private. It's not even on the sectionals. The runway is mowed grass 2200 feet by 50 feet with flat fields on either side. Plenty of room to learn on. We found out that we needed the room real quick.

The taxi tests were exciting, to say the least. Graham had warned us to be ready for the rudder to be ineffective at low speeds, and he was right. The first time I raised the tail, I did it too soon and promptly went from one side of the fifty foot runway to the other and only the presence of the super-duper brakes Tom had designed kept me from buying a runway marker. I stopped two feet away from the marker and missed tearing up the right lower wing by a hair.

As soon as my pulse went back to normal, I tried again. By bobbing from side to side in the cockpit and being very quick on the rudder, I was able to make the next runs straighter and faster. The secret is to let the tailwheel stay on the ground until the rudder becomes effective (about 20-25 mph) and then lift up. It sure is nice to be able to see the runway as the nose lowers and the vista appears before you. Once you get the tail up, she goes down the runway with a minimum of rudder stomping, and tracks like she is on rails.

The second day of taxi tests were calmer, now that we knew the ground handling characteristics of the Nieuports a little better. We weren't so nervous and could concentrate on what was happening instead of simply surviving. We started calling it the "Nieuport Shuffle" when we raised the tail too soon, and Tom and I both spent some time "weeding the soybeans" beside the runway. We hadn't installed the windshields yet and I knew Tom was having fun by the amount of bugs he had on his forehead and teeth. A happy pilot.

Mr. DeSalme called and said he would be out to inspect the birds on June 12. That set off a frenzy of final nit-picking preparations. My dad had finished carving the Lewis guns and they looked so real you expected them to shoot. We weren't going to install them until the first flights had shown us how we were going to have to trim the planes. Tom and I and our dads all went over each aircraft and looked for anything that we thought would make Mr. DeSalme's antennae wiggle, as we nervously awaited his arrival. He had also said that he would really like to see them fly, if they passed. That meant we had to do some more taxi testing to get even better acquainted with their ground handling characteristics.

The more we practiced, the better we got. By the third day of tests, we were able to keep a good straight line on the runway with the tail up in takeoff position. The torque of the VW engine was the opposite of the Continental on the Tweety Bird and I finally got used to pushing left rudder instead of right when the tail came up. If you ever get to see one of them fly, look for the "Nieuport Stomp" as the tail comes up.

June 12 came, and with it, Mr. DeSalme. He went over each plane with the proverbial fine tooth comb. There would be looooong silent periods while he was looking at things. Tom and I about died during those. We trailed him silently with the plans under one arm and our photo albums and records under the other. Sharon said we looked like two schoolboys following the professor around. He found four bolts he wanted us to safety and several placards we forgot to install. One was "PASSENGERS PROHIBITED." On a single-seater plane?

I looked at him kind of surprised and he said, "Don't say anything, just do it." I did.

There were a few places where we forgot to put slippage indicator paint spots on nuts and bolts. We did that. Then he turned to us and said, "They look real good. Button 'em up and push 'em out." (Oh, boy!)

We sprang into action with the grace and ease of a practiced Indy pit crew, and in 30 minutes they were ready to go. I told Tom in a non-negotiable way that I had to be the first to fly. We rolled Le Faucon Gris out of the hangar for her first time and both gave her an intense preflight. The wheels were blocked and Tom flipped the prop through a few times. I pulled my goggles down over my eyes and cracked the throttle open a quarter-inch.

"CONTACT!" Tom yelled.

"CONTACT!" I yelled back as I flipped the switch to "on." Tom swung the prop... nothing. He did it again.

She started on the second flip, and with the muffled bellow of the mighty Volkswagen as my accompaniment, I taxied out for my first "patrol."

There wasn't much to do at the end of the runway. We don't have two mags, so there is no mag check. (If you shut off the switch you get one heck of an rpm drop.) The only pre-takeoff check we have is "Fuel on." I had stalled as long as I could. I eased the throttle forward, the Volkswagen screamed and the Sterba prop dug in.

We rocketed down the runway. At 25 mph, I raised the tail, and it took only a little left rudder to keep her straight. When everything felt "good" (I didn't dare look down at the instrument panel to see what I was doing), I eased back on the stick and she lifted off as light as a feather. I held her straight ahead and gained about 50 feet of altitude as I felt out the aileron response. They worked great, so I pushed right and left rudder gently to check out directional control. No problem.

IT WAS JUST SWELL!! I had already noticed that I had to use back pressure on the stick to maintain level flight and knew the decallage was going to have to be changed from +1 degree to either 0 degrees or maybe even -1 to ease the pressure on the stick.* Other than that, SHE FLEW GREAT!!!! At 2500 rpm, the Volkswagen was hardly working and I was getting 55 to 60 mph indicated. (Once we got the engines broken in, we got a 3000 rpm cruise.) Seventy years rolled back as I roared over the fields, and I kept squinting up into the sun to see if any Fokkers were lurking up there.

After making gentle circuits of the field for about 20 minutes to see what my oil pressure and oil temperature were going to do, I went to 1500 feet AGL for my first stall. I couldn't put it off any longer. Keeping the wings level, I pulled the carb heat on and closed the throttle. The sound level dropped as I started easing the stick back. I was so nervous my feet were dancing on the rudder bar. When the airspeed passed below 40 mph, she still hadn't broken and I knew then that we had built a couple of sweeties.

At about 35-38 mph, I got a slight buffet and she broke gently straight ahead somewhere below 35 mph. The pitch-down was about 20 degrees. (At least that's what they told me it looked like from the ground. I thought I was going straight down.) I eased the stick forward, added power and she was flying again. I wanted to land then because I had found out all I needed to know on the first flight. I didn't want to do any more until we had adjusted the decallage in the stabilizer.

---

* Decallage is the difference in degrees between the line of the horizontal stabilizer and the incidence of the wing, if that helps any.

The landing was so simple it was anticlimactic. I set up a long final with power on, indicating 50 mph. I chopped power over the end of the runway and flared her onto a three-point landing(s). (Four bounces was the final consensus.) We landed and rolled about 100 feet with minimal rudder control needed. It wasn't going to take a lot to get her to fly hands-off. It would have taken a surgeon to take the grin off my face. She flew better than my wildest dreams.

Then it was Tom's turn. He picked my brains about my flight and the only thing I could tell him was to be ready to hold back pressure on the stick, and that he would probably need more than I did because his CG is about one inch ahead of mine.

His engine started on about the tenth crank and he taxied out to commit aviation. When his tail came up he veered to the right and headed straight for a landing light. It became dead silent on the flight line as we watched the disaster unfold. Tom veered to the right even more and missed the landing light. Now he was headed straight for the soybeans. (I think green growing things in a rough field are like a magnet to Tom when he is in a plane.) His wife was moaning softly and Mr. DeSalme was muttering, "Whoa boy, whoa!" as we watched Tom rushing towards the bean field.

Just as the Nieuport was about to transform itself into a John Deere, Tom hauled the stick back and ended up just running the bottom half of his wheels through the tops of the first rows of plants. All of us on the ground expelled great gasps of air as she lifted up out of the plants' greedy green grasp.

The rest of his flight was the same as mine. We had about a five mph crosswind and it was coming over the bluffs to the west of the airport, so there was a lot of "burbulence" on final approach. Tom made one run down the runway to feel out the conditions and then we saw him line up for the "Big One." He did a beautiful three pointer and didn't roll 75 feet. His stick pressure was a lot greater than mine, and we decided to adjust the decallage of the stabs before we did any more flying. Besides that, we were pooped from the release of tension.

The planes were hauled into the hangar. Mr. DeSalme gave us our restricted flight area chart for our 40 hours of testing. We presented him with one of our "Dawn Patrol" patches and a certificate that he was now an Honorary Flight Lieutenant in the Dawn Patrol. (He still calls me and wants to talk and I still go up to the FSDO to say howdy about once a month. He was very helpful through the whole building process and I am sure we couldn't have done it without his assistance.)

Then the hidden cooler of beer and champagne was pulled out. (We were through flying for the day.) The bucket of Extra Crispy was torn open and the celebration began to gather steam. After 16 months of toil and sweat, blood and tears, despair and joy and hours of confusion, the planes were done, inspected and flown! Hooray!!

* * *

The next day we tweaked the decallage in the stabs 1 ½ degrees. Then we both made some short test flights to see if any further changes were needed. They weren't. The stick pressure was "hands off" for pitch and roll at 2600 rpm and 65 mph. The only thing that still had us concerned was the tendency for the plane to "Dutch roll" to the right from engine torque when you took your feet off the rudder pedals. Reducing the throttle to idle took engine torque out of the picture and solved the rudder problem, but it also meant that if you somehow lost rudder control in the air you had to go down right then, because if you kept power on you would auger in.

I landed, fabricated a quick and dirty trim tab, attached it to the lower ventral fin with 400 mph tape, and took off. She was perfect! Hands and feet off with power on. The roll was gone and when I reduced power she still acted docile. Now I had what I wanted – a hands off, no pressure, inherently stable aircraft. She was ready for the world.

The next month was a wild and crazy time. Every night and all day on weekends we were out flying the planes and tweaking the wing wires and tail decallage until they were just perfect. We put the 40 hours required by Mr. DeSalme on the planes in just over a month. It was a real ordeal, but we wanted to have them well broken in for the Oshkosh odyssey.

We didn't know then how many adventures we were going to have before going to Oshkosh that year. We also didn't know that the FAA was going to throw one more frustrating length of red tape at us.

The Data Plate

We triumph over bureaucracy.

"I'M NOT GOING TO DO IT!" Tom screamed. "IT'S JUST SOME MORE GOVERNMENT BUREAUCRATIC POO-POO FROM A MALE BOVINE! (Or words to that effect). His face was mottled red and white, his eyes glared and his shaking hands clutched the arms of his lawn chair in a death grip. I knew his safety valve was stuck wide open. I'd seen this before. At times like this, logic and reason flew out the window and emotions ran high.

"Tom," I said, "If we don't do it, we can't go to any fly-ins, air shows or even other airports. Hell, if an inspector comes to our airport, looks at the planes and doesn't see it, he could ground us and fine us for being illegal. We're going to have to do it."

Tom was still agitated. "This just stinks. Here we try to paint our planes to look authentic and those *#*&% ^ & do this to us!"

We both stared glumly at the paper before us. It was an official notice from the FAA that said that all aircraft had to have a "data plate" attached to the rear of the fuselage, port side, aft of the door and visible from the ground, stating the make, model and serial number of the aircraft. It was the latest in a series of moves designed, I think, to make it easier for the feds to identify and track drug runners. How anybody with a brain larger than one cell could think that our little Nieuport 11 replicas could run drugs escaped me. When you cruise at 60, have a V_{ne} (Velocity Never Exceed) of 85, and possess a glide angle like a rock, your chances of being high on a drug runner's list of favorite transport aircraft are nil and none. Boy, did this grate!

The first thing I had to do was calm Tom down. Over the years I had found out the perfect method. I reached down into the cooler, pulled out a frosty beer, popped the top and handed it to him. He took a long healthy pull, sighed, and leaned back in his chair. The color in his face started to recede. I knew he was ready to listen to reason. We were sitting in the hangar beside the planes. It was raining and the drumming on the tin roof was a soothing roar in the background.

I hated as much as Tom did the rule we had just received. As usual, there was no way out. We had to do it. Just like we had to have the placard "PASSENGERS PROHIBITED" prominently displayed in our little, cramped, one-holer planes. Tom read the letter again. I sat glumly trying to figure out where to place the disfiguring anachronistic plate on our authentic-looking WWI planes.

Time passed. The rain was a soothing drone on the roof. I slowly started to nod and fell into a peaceful snooze. I am a master of the quick nap.

"I'VE GOT IT!" Tom suddenly yelled.

I sat up in my chair with a jerk. "Hey!" I cried, "What's with the yelling?" Tom looked at me with a smile on his face. "These are French planes right?" "Yeah, so what?" I answered.

"Read this sucker again." he commanded, handing me the letter.

I read it and then looked at him wonderingly. "So?"

"Is there anywhere in there where it says the make, model and serial number have to be in English?" he inquired with a grin.

I read it again. Then, we both read it one more time. We looked at each other with broad smiles on our ugly faces.

"Nope" I said. "I'll get right on it."

My first call when I got home was to the high school French teacher. She knew me well from when we were trying to think of names for our planes, and when she heard who it was on the phone she said, "Oh for gawdsake, what do you two idiots want now?" I told her and had the information in a few minutes. Then I ran down to the local office supply store and bought a supply of one-inch stick-on letters. It took about an hour of effort, grinning and giggling, and the job was done. We were legal again! There, standing tall and proud on the side of my fuselage, were the resounding phrases:

FAISEUR D'AVION - STARKS
DÉSIGNATION DE MODELS D'AVION - NIEUPORT 11
PARISSANT PER NUMEROS D'AVION - 36

Yessiree, make, model and serial number. Just like the letter demanded. Right there on the side of the plane. Legible from the ground. *In French!*

We went to an air show about a month later. We were asked to fly the Nieuports in a fly-by display. The FAA guy overseeing the air show inspected all our papers and logs to make sure everything was legal. Then he wandered over to look at the planes. Tom and I watched in gleeful anticipation as he walked around the Nieuports and checked them out. He got to the port side and stopped, stunned. He read the data plate under the Lafayette Escadrille Indian head insignias. Then he looked at Tom and me as we stood there grinning at him. I handed him the official letter. He read it and handed it back.

"Nice touch." He smiled and ambled on down the line. We'd done it! Once again, Science and Technology had triumphed over Bureaucratic Baloney.

IV

More Aerial Adventures

The Dawn Patrol's First Mission

Actually, a lot of firsts.

The first real test of the Nieuports was to be the "Operation Handshake" air show at Richards-Gebauer Air Base on July 19th and 20th in Kansas City. The officer in charge told me he would like to have the Nieuports attend. Tom couldn't make it Saturday, so I was going to be the only representative of the Dawn Patrol for the first day of the show. I had just gotten my new handheld radio and had never even tried it out. It was also going to be the first time the plane had ever flown onto a hard-surfaced runway. It was its first cross-country, too. A lot of firsts. I was nervous. What if I made one of my famous "squat-and-leave-it" landings at a big air show in front of a big crowd? I would just light a match to the wreckage and walk away.

The 30-mile flight to the air base took 45 minutes into the teeth of a 15-knot headwind. (Sharon drove, and probably made better time than I did.) I was about 15 miles out when I called the tower to tell them I was coming in.

"Richards-Gebauer Tower, Nieuport One Two Four Delta Sierra... " Long silence... "Richards-Gebauer Tower, Nieuport One Two Four Delta Sierra... "

"Aircraft calling Richards-Gebauer Tower, say again." I did, and there was another long silence...

"One Two Four Delta Sierra... say again your aircraft type... " I did.

"One Two Four Delta Sierra... say aircraft type again."

"November One Two Four Delta Sierra is a Nieuport Eleven." There was another long silence. He finally came back and gave me the numbers and told me to report back when I was on a two-mile right base for runway one-eight.

I chugged along for about five minutes and then the tower called back and asked my position. I told him I was three miles further along than last time. Another long silence ensued. This time he asked me what a Nieuport Eleven was. I told him it was a warbird. This led to a real looooong silence. Ten minutes later I reported a two-mile right base for one-eight and he cleared me to land. Right after he did that, a Beechcraft and Piper called in and he told them they were numbers two and three to land. I had reduced my speed to 45 mph and was thrashing right along, fat, dumb and happy. As it turned out, all three of us ended up on final at the same time, and when the smoke had cleared, I was the last one to land.

As I was taxiing in, the tower controller got a good look at me and finally understood what he had been coping with. We had a good chuckle and he ended up coming down to chat with me and look at the Nieuport when he got off shift.

The reception I got at the air show was a preview of what Oshkosh was going to be like. There was a crowd three deep around the plane at all times and I never did get a chance to go sniffing around the other exhibits, because I couldn't get away from all the people asking questions.

Two of the planes flying in the air show were the F-14 Tomcat and F-15 Eagle. The first couple of hours of the show were for wandering around and looking at all the planes on display. I was standing by the Nieuport when someone called out, "Hey, Mr. Starks!" I turned around, and there was this tall, good-looking man in a Navy flight suit standing outside the rope around the Nieuport. "Remember me?" he queried.

I didn't have the foggiest idea who he was, so I looked down at his flight suit at his name patch and saw the name, Tim Cowden. Geeze, how they change! He was a kid I had taught in seventh grade math fourteen years back. I looked closer and saw that he was an RIO (Radar Information Officer) on an F-14 Tomcat. His nickname/call sign was AWOL. (He stood on the pier once and watched the ship sail off without him.) We talked for a while and then I found out he had been to Top Gun school and was one of the extras in the movie. (I had seen it only four times, but made it a fifth two days later and spotted him in two scenes.)

We swapped some good-ole-days talk for a while and then he asked if he could please sit in the Nieuport. It took a while for that question to register. Here was a guy who regularly flies around in one of the Navy's meanest $43 million high-tech fighters and he wants to sit in my little $3,000 60-mile-per-hour Volkswagen-powered, wooden-machine-gun-armed, bicycle-wheel landing-geared, slow-as-a-snail... HELL, YES! HE COULD SIT IN THE PLANE!!!

One minute later he was in the cockpit, and I was taking pictures as fast as I could wind the camera. Sharon and I both had to have our pictures taken with him. I might add at this time that Tim is the type that my little eighth grade girls would call a "superhunk." Maybe that explains the momentary period of insanity that suddenly took control of my normally quiet, demure, shy wife. She was squirming and giggling like a teenie-bopper in front of a rock star. First she wanted to have her picture taken with him. Then she wanted to hug him. Then Sharon just had to kiss him and he had to kiss her. It was nauseating. I almost barfed. (For three weeks after that, whenever I would give her a pinch, a squeeze and a leer, she would throw a brick at me.)

Tim and I had a real nice long talk, and I am glad we have guys like him guarding our skies. He gave us pictures he had taken of a Russian Bear Bomber the F-14s were escorting somewhere over the ocean. Tim came back to see us again and again during the course of the air show. I was proud to be able to point him out to other air show patrons and tell them I used to teach that naval officer decimals and fractions.

After Tim had left, I had my next big thrill. I looked up and saw another flight-suit-clad figure looking at the Nieuport. He was Major Brian Badger, the F-15 Eagle demonstration pilot at the air show. Major Badger asked me a lot of questions about the history of the Nieuport and how we had built the Dawn Patrol. Then he asked if *he* could sit in the Nieuport. Hot Damn! Two in one day!

One minute later, Major Badger was in the cockpit with my six-foot white silk scarf around his neck and my goggles over his eyes. He was working the stick and rudder bar and reaching up to pull the trigger on the replica Lewis 303 machine gun. It was while he was sitting there, squinting through the gun sight, that he muttered in a low voice, "You know, I've never wanted to fly a prop plane until now."

I just couldn't relate to that and was struck silent for a few minutes. (Major Badger came back to see us and the Nieuport both days of the air show and gave us some beautiful autographed pictures of the Eagle with motivational messages written to our different math classes. He is another man that I am glad is guarding our skies. Men like Tim Cowden and Brian Badger are a hell of a lot better role models for the youth of today than some of the rock stars and sports "heroes" who are always in the news. We need more like them. Two weeks after the air show, Sharon and I both received very nice letters from Major Badger addressed to our math classes, exhorting them to do their best in school. Needless to say, those letters are now encased in plastic and mounted on our bulletin boards for all to see and read.)

When I was taxiing out to leave the air show on Sunday afternoon, I passed the Thunderbirds lined up in their area. I was struck by the enormous difference that 70 years could make in military aviation development. One of the crew members working on the F-16s saw me, did a double-take, snapped to attention, and gave me and Le Faucon Gris a sharp salute. It was one of the high points of the air show for me.

The wind was from 360 degrees at 14 knots, and the active runway was 36. Just as I took the active, I felt a rumbling vibration in the tail and looked back just in time to see the plastic tread on the hardware store caster I was using for a tailwheel fall off the hub. We were rolling on the hub just fine, so I said the heck with it and departed when they said to.

When I took off, I was climbing out at 40 mph indicated into the 14 knot head wind. For a while, I thought I was going backwards. I was feeling like Snidley J. Whiplash chasing Fokkers until the tower brought me back to earth. Someone in a Cessna said he was ready to go and the tower said, "Ahhhhh... Cessna 412 Delta... taxi into position and hold... you'll have to wait a while. We have some very, very slow traffic departing at the present time on runway heading." (That peckerwood was talking about me!!)

I called them back and said, "This is the very, very slow traffic, and I will be glad to turn if you want me to." He thanked me and told me to expedite same. I made a 90 degree turn to the left, waited a minute and turned back to the north. I counted five planes taking off before I reached the end of the runway. (It was a heck of a long runway.) Maybe I am slow, but I know I'm having a lot more fun than they are.

The next week was spent getting both birds ready for the big 478-mile trip to Oshkosh. Tom and I each checked everything twice on our own plane and then switched and did the same to each other's plane. We were ready. Look out, Oshkosh! Here comes the Dawn Patrol!!!

Unhappy End

A tail of woe.

The three days prior to our departure on the 31st were clear and sunny, with a southwest wind. Our course to Oshkosh is about 40 degrees magnetic, and we were rubbing our hands together at the prospect of a tailwind.

When the alarm blared me out of bed at 3:30 in the morning and I heard the wind roaring in the trees outside the bedroom, I smiled. It was too dark to see what was going on when Tom picked me up at 4:00, so we called flight service; it was like having a bucket of ice-cold water thrown over us. One thousand foot ceilings, visibility three miles in fog and haze, and the wind from 360 at 15 knots, and that was at ground level. We decided to go to the airport and see if conditions would improve.

They didn't. We rolled the Nieuports out, preflighted them, and sat down to wait at 6:00 for the weather to improve. By 7:00, we could at least see that the clouds were broken and we could spot the grain elevator five miles away, so we decided if we were ever going to get there we had better go.

Our planes lifted off at 7:13 A.M., and we headed north, scud-running around the Kansas City TCA. Tom was leading. I had the chart and was inching my finger along it as we crept onward and Tom was looking for checkpoints. He kept asking me if there were any towers coming up on the chart. The ceiling was still about 1500 feet AGL, but the air was smooth. My rear end was sending its first messages of incredulous surprise to my brain about the abuse it was going through and promising more and greater agony if this treatment continued.

Our first leg was 90 miles to Trenton, Missouri. The first checkpoint on my flight plan was Smithville Lake, a distance of 30 miles. We were indicating about 70 mph, so I figured we'd hit it in about 25 minutes. When it finally showed up, 49 minutes later, I knew we were in big trouble. We were getting 37 mph ground speed. The smart thing to do would have been to turn back.

We pressed on. (No one has ever accused either Tom or me of having a surplus of smarts.) After Smithville Lake, we were going to follow I-35 to Gallatin, turn right and pick up the railroad tracks into Trenton. It was IFRR flying at its most basic, along with IFIS (I Fly InterStates). We thrashed our way up the Interstate, keeping it to our left, following the unwritten rule of air navigation that says that, even in the air, you still drive on the right side of the road.

We had CB radios in our planes and were blabbering away steadily, comparing where we were on the chart. Suddenly, a voice broke in on the little-used channel we were chattering on.

"Breaker Breaker, channel one for them-thar airplanes up there."

I grinned and picked up my mike. "Go ahead, Breaker."

"Who I got up there?" the voice asked. "Come back." ("Come back" is the CB equivalent of "over.")

I answered him. "Hey there, good buddy. You got the one and only Dawn Patrol up here trucking our way north on Eye-Three-Five. Come back."

The next few moments were used to exchange handles (CB call signs). I'm the Gray Falcon and Tom is the Silver Slug.

I might digress here for a minute and explain the term "Good Buddy" for those infinitesimal few of you who have never eavesdropped on the fascinating and educational dissertations you can hear over the Citizen Band radio channels. Everybody is your "Good Buddy."

Sharon and I were out on the Interstate one day when two citizens got into a rather lively altercation over the radio. I can't tell you exactly what they called each other but they both got rather graphic in their threats of bodily harm. The discussion reached its climax with one of them telling the other that he would meet him at mile marker 56 and, at that location, he was going to wrest the CB radio forcefully from the other combatant's vehicle and relocate it in a place where I seriously doubt it would fit without causing extreme discomfort.

Well, let me tell you, Sharon and I are not ones to ignore an entertainment opportunity like that, so, when we got to mile marker 56, we pulled off and waited. There were about 20 others parked there who had also been listening in on the heated exchange. We all waited patiently for events to develop. After about five minutes two *big* rigs drove up and two extremely large, angry, hairy, gorilla-like individuals got out. The resulting altercation was short but intense. The expected transfer of the radio did not develop, but the proceedings exceeded anything that televised wrestling could ever display. And up until the first punch was thrown, they were still calling each other "Good Buddy." Isn't human nature a monumental riddle? We drove on refreshed and entertained.

Anyway, back to The Dawn Patrol's trial by fire. Our good buddy was going up I-35 North the same way we were, and wanted to know our 10-20 (location). I told him we were five miles south of Gallatin and heading north. He called back all excited and said he was on the same stretch of road we were. He described his rig to us and asked if we could find him. We looked for the red tanker and, sure enough, there he was, rapidly running away from us, heading north.

Then he said, "Hey there, good buddies, would'ja run mah front door for me and shake the trees?" That meant he wanted us to look up ahead and tell him if there were any Smokey Bears (Highway Patrol cars) up ahead who would give him Green Stamps (speeding tickets).

I came back and told him, "Hey there, good buddy, you just passed us and will be outta sight in five minutes. We've got the pedal to the metal in these suckers and can't go any faster."

The silence that resulted from that transmission was eloquent in its disbelief. He finally came back on and asked what kind of planes we were and how fast were we flying. When I told him, there was another long silence and then he said, "Well, it's been nice jawing atcha." Two plumes of black smoke shot up from his exhaust stacks and away he went.

Just about then we spotted the railroad tracks we were going to follow from Gallatin to Trenton. I picked up the CB mike and in my best John Wayne voice screamed, "TROOP! COLUMN RIGHT! HO!"

Tom yelled back, "HO!"

Our two canvas falcons banked right and thundered onward into the gloom. While following the railroad tracks up to Trenton, we were passed by two slow freight trains. It was a prelude to the ultimate humiliation we were to suffer later. The trip was already becoming a legend.

The landings at Trenton were no problem, since the runway runs north/south. We landed at 9:23. It had taken 2.2 hours to go 80 miles. Thirty seven mph average groundspeed — and no relief in sight. The wind felt like it was even stronger in Trenton than in K. C.

Our arrival in Trenton was where we got our first inkling of the response the Nieuports were going to get wherever we went. As we were rolling in, cars started driving up and people came running with cameras in their hands. We were planning on a 15-minute stop, but between answering questions, posing for pictures, fueling up, and rubbing our rears, it took a lot longer. The planes took 6.9 gallons each, and our guesstimates about our fuel consumption were confirmed. About 3 gallons per hour.

We cranked them up and departed Trenton at 9:52 and headed up the railroad tracks to Ottumwa, Iowa. Visibility was about 15 miles now, and our checkpoints were visible for a long time. We experienced no further navigation problems for the rest of the day. The wind was still blowing hard, and from 3500 feet you could see the trees whipping around and throwing leaves, branches, and bird nests out. The air at 3500 was still smooth; however, it sure seemed like we were going even slower than the first leg. My rear was sending even more insistent demands to cease the torture, and it was starting to look like a very long day. Boring, too.

Tom was still leading and I was following our trail on the chart and calling out checkpoints. Just then, I flew through a smell that threatened to take the paint off the plane. I immediately called Tom on the radio and asked him if he had done something bad in his plane. He told me to look down. That's when I discovered that you can smell a pig farm at 2500 feet AGL on a windy day.

We soon discovered another thrill of flying in an open cockpit airplane: trying to fold the charts. The first time I tried it, the chart

We soon discovered another thrill of flying in an open cockpit airplane: trying to fold the charts.

wrapped around my head and I almost lost it and the plane during the resulting wrestling match. From then on, whenever I needed to go over another fold in the chart, I would call over to Tom to fly at least a quarter of a mile away while I did it. Tom said I did almost all of the maneuvers in the aerobatic handbook while I was folding the chart. I really wouldn't know. The only way I could fold the chart was to duck down in the cockpit, swell up like an angry toad to fill as much of the hole as possible, hold the chart down by the floor near the rudder bar and then try to fold it. I did such a good job that I generally had to buy a new chart at every other stop.

The airport at Ottumwa finally came into view and we got into the pattern. The wind was 15 knots across the runway at 70 degrees with gusts to 20. The Nieuports land so slow and the runway was so wide that I just landed across the runway and was stopped before I got to the other side. That was our first experience with the crosswind component capabilities of the Nieuports. If it's too high, land across. We did it several times at different airports on the trip. We shut the engines off at Ottumwa at 12:19 P.M. Ninety-two miles in 2.4 hours. Ground speed... a blazing 37.5 mph. It was definitely going to be a looooong day. We filled the planes up, posed for a few pictures, and headed for the Flight Service Station to see if the winds would be the same all the way to Oshkosh. We staggered in the door, rubbing our rear ends and groaning. The weather briefer looked at us, and said, "Are you the guys who just came in with the two WWI planes?"

We said we were and he looked stern and said, "Well, you can't leave for a little while."

I immediately wondered what FAR we had fractured on our way here and was prepared to throw myself down at his feet and plead for mercy. "What did we do wrong?" I quavered while keeping a strong grip on Tom, who was trying to sneak out the door and leave me.

Then his face split in a big grin and he started to laugh and said, "I'd really appreciate it if you could wait until my wife gets up here with the camera. I called her as soon as I saw you guys land and she's bringing it up here as fast as she can."

We had a nice talk with him and he steered us to the airport restaurant, where we took on metabolic fuel and let our poor abused rear ends enjoy a cushioned seat. The air was starting to get bumpy and a 172 pilot sitting beside us said the winds at 3500 feet were 30 knots from the north. He was all disgusted and bent out of shape because it had taken him a whole two and one half hours to get from Kansas City to Ottumwa. Since it had taken us 4.6 hours to cover the same distance, we weren't too sympathetic an audience. We left him muttering into his milk shake and went to start up the torture chambers for the next exciting leg of the trip.

We already knew we were going to have to go in 80- to 90-mile legs with the groundspeed we were getting, and our rears were also going to be a limiting factor. Mine started to whimper when I sat down in the plane. I don't know how those fighter pilots in the Thunderbolts and Mustangs ever made those five- and six-hour deep penetration raids into Europe during WWII, sitting on a parachute and life raft with a CO_2 bottle embedded in them.

We fired up the planes at 1:45 and set out for Iowa City, a short leg of only 60 miles. We decided to stay low and buck the turbulence at about a thousand feet AGL in order to get less headwind. It worked. We got to Iowa city in one hour and 15 minutes. WOW!! A whopping 48 mph ground speed. Now we're really moving. We got there at 3:00 and did a quick fuel-up and headed on to Dubuque, a 70-mile hop.

It was on this leg that we suffered the supreme humiliation: we got passed by a dump truck — a *full* dump truck — on a gravel road. It was a new low in aviation history.

My bottom was now screaming urgent messages to my brain about the abuse, so I loosened my straps and tried to find a position that would ease the agony. I sat first on one hip and then the other. I leaned forward and back. I even lifted myself up by my elbows on the cockpit rim and tried to let everything fall back into its usual plump shape. Nothing worked. I was dying. We thrashed into Dubuque at 5:00. I fell out of the plane, crawled over to Tom, grabbed his pants leg and started to plead. I just couldn't go any further.

Besides the problems with my poor abused rear end, the wind was worse; our groundspeed was starting to go down again. We had averaged 44 mph on the leg and Oshkosh was still 155 miles away. We couldn't go any further. We were standing around with our chins quivering and looking like two whipped pups, when one of aviation's guardian angels stepped up. It was William J. Hanley, a flight instructor at Dubuque. He listened to our tale of woe, pointed out the fuel truck, and walked off. We refueled the planes and were thinking of how we were going to spend the night on the couches in the lounge when William came walking back.

He smiled, "Okay, guys, I've got you both hangar space for the night and reserved you a room in a close, clean, family-run motel." Then he dropped a set of car keys in Tom's hand. "Here's the keys to my other car. Just park her outside when you leave in the morning." He smiled and left us there with our eyes bugged out and our mouths hanging open. We had heard about Good Samaritans, but it was the first time we had ever met one. He showed up at Oshkosh and we thanked him again there, but I would like to do it again now... THANKS!!

We grabbed a bite and hit the sacks. I had to sleep on my stomach because by then I believed I had done permanent, severe damage to my tail. I was sure that I could feel bone chips grinding around every time I moved.

We hauled out at 5:30 in the morning and got ready for the first of two legs to Oshkosh: Dubuque to Morey Field near Madison, and then on to Wittman.

We drove the car to the airport, parked it where Bill had told us to, and left his keys with the friendly people at the desk. They wished us a safe trip and told us to come back soon.

The planes had to be hand started, and it was becoming very apparent that we would have to add starters as soon as we had enough money in the till. Tom's plane started on the first flip, and as it idled, tied down, we got ready to try and start mine. Thirty minutes later, we were both standing there with our tongues hanging out and too tired to even cuss. That %&$#$% was flooded so bad that raw gas was running out of the exhaust pipes. We knew from bitter experience that this was going to be one of those days from then on.

By shutting the gas off, opening the throttle, shutting the switch off, and cranking the prop backwards at least 50 times, we would get the engine to give a few feeble little "poof-poof-poofs" when cranked. Then we would go through the whole backwards cranking and cussing routine again. On the third try she finally started. By then, my heart was threatening to burst from my chest, and I was feeling just a tad sickie-poo. We still had a long way to go.

I punched in the tower frequency of Dubuque and started calling them to see if they would let us go. I called and called and called. No answer. Tom was jabbering on the CB, asking me what was the holdup, and I was alternately trying to calm him and raise the tower and had mike cords all over the cockpit. Just about then, one of the line crew finally quit laughing long enough to come out and tell us that the tower didn't open for another hour and we had been calling on a dead frequency for about ten minutes. We taxied out and took the active and got ready to take off for the last two legs of what was rapidly becoming an odyssey.

We departed Dubuque at 6:50 and headed for Morey Field, just west of Madison, Wisconsin. We had another headwind, naturally. Visibility was an unbelievable thirty miles, so we decided to drop our road/railroad/water tower/road sign navigation and do it right. We figured out a compass course and headed out at 040 degrees +/-20 degrees for wind. The leg was 73 miles, and we plopped into Morey Field at 8:20. Groundspeed... 49 mph. Morey is a delightful field on the outskirts of Madison and is worth the visit. While Tom wasn't looking, I got out the new six-foot white silk flying scarf with the Army Air Corps insignia that Sharon had bought me and wrapped it around my neck for the last leg of the trip. I wanted to arrive in style.

A quick fuel up and away we went. We left Morey at 8:50 and staggered upward. We got over Waupun, and I could see Wittman from there. The visibility was fantastic. We spotted a gaggle of warbirds forming up over Lake Winnebago. Then we got to Fond Du Lac and started up the railroad track that we had to follow on the No Radio Arrival instruction sheet. The wind was from about 330 degrees at 14 knots, and the big orange arrow showed that the runway in use for No Radio Arrivals was 36L. I went in first, waggled my wings on base as the instructions said, and lined up for my landing. There was no traffic in the pattern, but it looked like a *big* flock of planes were off to the west, getting ready to get in the pattern for 36L too. My rear was already starting to quiver in anticipation of no more agony.

I was so excited I was panting and my feet were shaking on the rudder bar as I started my flare. I made one of my better arrivals, which means no parts fell off the plane. I landed across the runway and went off into the grass as soon as I could. I pulled my white silk scarf out of my jacket and arranged it so it would flutter gallantly out behind me. I waited for Tom to come up beside me so we could taxi in together, covered in glory.

I waited... and waited... and waited. My straps were too tight for me to turn around and see what was going on, but I found out soon enough. Tom's disgusted voice suddenly came through my earphones. "Dick... I broke a wheel."

Oh, for cripes' sakes! I knew what he meant. We had already broken two of the motor-cross bicycle wheels we were using during our taxi-testing and knew from hard experience that, while the wheels could take an enormous vertical load, they couldn't take any high side stresses without breaking.

I loosened my straps and turned around in the cockpit. A hard-to-describe, panoramic view greeted my distended eyes. There was Tom's Nieuport, looking like a ruptured duck, leaning drunkenly on its right landing gear leg on the right side of the runway. A solitary, hubless wheel lay in shattered splendor in the middle of the runway. A P-51 was sucking its gear up and clawing for altitude, its Merlin engine bellowing as it started its go-around. A Stinson flashed by on the right. A Mooney streaked by on the left. Behind him, it looked like a demented flock of sparrows as planes scattered to the four winds, seeking less dangerous places to land.

I figured the controllers in the tower were already boiling the oil to dump Tom and me in for what we had done to their beautifully orchestrated landing pattern. We had to get the debris cleared away and I mean right now!

I threw off my straps and leaped out of my cockpit — into about six inches of icy water. My only shoes, too. I then remembered the newscast about the frog strangler that Oshkosh had endured the night before, and reconciled myself to four days of wet, wrinkled, and stinky feet at Oshkosh. What a way to start a trip.

I ran over to Tom and we tried to figure out how to move the plane off the runway. With me lifting up the right wing raising the gear leg off the ground, and Tom pushing the plane, we were able to get her off to the west side of the runway. Just about then, some guy came running up, shook Tom's hand and said, "Welcome to Oshkosh."

Tom was too shocked and tired to do anything but stare at him. He was trying to see if the plane had sustained any other damage besides a shattered wheel and a bent axle. Rescuers were starting to arrive.

(One of the first helpers to get to us was Brent Weathered, an ex-student of mine. Brent has changed from the skinny little eighth-grader of 18 years back. Now he's six-foot-nine and about 280 pounds. I call him "Mongo." Everyone else calls him "Sir!")

It was too far to move the plane by lifting up the wing and pushing, so we decided to do some wheel trading. We pushed my plane up to the WWI aircraft parking area, took off the right wheel, and ran back to Tom's plane. With the wheel on, the plane was moved to sit beside mine. We had arrived! I would have kissed the ground, except it was so muddy.

The next day and a half were a lesson in what being in the EAA is all about. We had so many people asking — no, begging — to help us, we had to say no to a lot of them.

I kept telling Tom, "Buddy, if you had to bend the bird, you sure did pick the right place to do it!" I shudder to think of the delay we would have had if we had to do the repairs anywhere else. EAA'ers are sooooo nice.

We straightened the axle by using the Dawn Patrol's flabtralic press. I am the flabtralic press. This is in reference to my physique. Some unkind people have said I resemble a pear with legs. Tom and Mongo held the bent axle in position while I jumped up and down on it until it was straight. All this knuckle-crunching exertion was accompanied by a purple cloud of profanity. Finally, everything was tweaked to our satisfaction. Time to repair: one and one-half days.

Mongo disappeared while we were finishing up the repairs on the wheel and reappeared an hour later with a real smug grin on his face. He had trudged up to the fly market and bought Tom a Ground Loop Certificate. We all got together and signed it, and Mongo presented it to Tom in an appropriate award ceremony. Not very many mortals have held up traffic at the world's busiest airport for five minutes and lived to tell about it. It is now permanently mounted in a glass-faced frame on Tom's trophy wall.

We were so busy at Oshkosh fixing Tom's plane that we were only vaguely aware of the crowds that were always clustered around the Nieuports. One of the biggest attractions about the little jewels is the fact that we built them for less that $3,000 each. In these times of $10,000 ultralights, and $40,000 to $80,000 kit planes, the Circa Nieuport is like a breath of fresh air to the common man who wants to fly. I don't think that you can get much more common than Tom and me. We can take cheap and turn it into an art form.

* * *

We were able to stay at Oshkosh for only three days because Tom had to get back to work. Monday, we fired the planes up at 7:30 A.M., roared off the ultralight runway, made a fly-by for the folks in the ultralight area and headed off southwest. The wind was out of the southwest, so once again, naturally, we had a headwind. This time we were ready. We had our course set up for short legs and were prepared to bounce our guts out at low altitude to get some groundspeed.

The trip from Oshkosh all the way to Ottumwa was slow and uneventful. Visibility was good and the winds were steady. The short legs and low altitude plan worked like a charm, and each leg was only about an hour to an hour and a half for 70 to 80 miles. It was basically very boring. We never got lost, I had a big cushion for my rear, the charts were prefolded, and visibility was good.

The boredom ended at Ottumwa. We landed in a light shower. The rain quit while we were refueling, but the sky was sullen looking, with a great big dark greenish-purple area to the northwest. Four air traffic controllers I know from classroom visits to an air traffic control class at the Kansas City International Control Tower rolled up in a Beechcraft on their way to Oshkosh. They said that the weather back towards Kansas City was scattered very light showers, "No problem, easy VFR." We looked at the hanging, swollen-looking gray skies and the real dark ominous area to the northwest of Ottumwa and flipped a coin. Heads... we go; tails... we flip again. Heads... finally! Off we went into the lowering haze.

We flew a zig-zag course to Trenton. We'd fly west until we hit rain and then fly kind of southwest along the edge of the curtain of rain until we could see through it. (Sucker hole.) We'd then thrash our way through the hole, pop into the clear, find some railroad tracks, go to the next town, read the water tower, find out where we were on the chart and zig-zag our way onward. I couldn't believe the number of towns named Water District. As we were splashing through one of the heavier showers, hiding behind the windshields to keep from getting the skin flayed off our face, a thought came to me.

"Hey, Tom," I yelled into my CB, "Did you waterproof our distributor caps?" (The distributor sits out front and is in the airstream.) There was a long silence.

Then he came back. "Keep your eyes peeled for emergency fields."

I wasn't bored any more. Every time I saw rain on the windshield from then on, my pucker factor would get so high I could have done aerobatics without a seat belt and not fallen out. We had one more bad stretch of rain and then broke through the line of storms and saw the sun shining in front of us all the way to the horizon. We landed at Trenton at 6:00 P.M., refueled, and were off for our last 80 miles at 6:30.

The last bit of excitement on the trip took place about half-way home. I was thrashing along in the lead and Tom was about 300 feet off my right wing at my four o'clock position. His voice suddenly came in my earphones. "Bandit, seven o'clock high, closing fast." (We like to talk military when we are on patrol.)

I swiveled around in my seat and watched a retractable something-or-other go flashing by off my left wing. He circled around and came back by with his flaps down, trying to slow to our speed. No luck. Then he circled around behind us again, lowered his gear and, with every-thing down and dirty and hanging on the prop, he was able to wallow along with us. As he came by on our left again, I was able to see the person in the right seat cranking a camera as fast as he could push the button. I waved, he waved, I gave a wing wiggle, he gave us a wing wiggle, sucked everything hanging out back up, rapidly accelerated, and left us in his dust. I wonder if he thought he was caught in some kind of time warp when he first saw us.

At 7:55 P.M., we shut the engines off at our home field. It had taken 11.5 hours to fly up to Oshkosh and 10.7 hours to fly back. Average ground speed... 43 mph. The only thing that saved me and my rear on the trip home was the Temperfoam cushion I bought at Oshkosh. (It did everything they said it would, and I recommend it to anyone with a similar problem.)

As the props shuddered to a stop, the throaty thunder of the mighty Volkswagen 1700cc engines gave way to the silence that usually rules the Missouri River bottoms. This was quickly replaced by the shrill whine as the first squadron of vicious mosquitoes dove in for the at-tack. Tom and I just sat in the cockpits, swatting and staring at each other in disbelief and relief. It was over. We had survived. We had years and years of beer drinking, tall tales, lies and reminiscing in front of us. (That's what miserable experiences are all about.) We got out of the planes and put them in the hangar. Tom came up to me and held out his hand.

"Well, buddy, we made it. I had a good time," he said as we shook hands. Then he walked around behind me and kicked me in my poor abused butt. "And that's for scaring the @%@# out of me in the rain, you @#$@&$%#, when you asked me about the distributors," he screamed at me. He got very abusive and called into question my family heritage, personal habits, said my mother probably barked and had fleas, and that I was very likely sitting in the church scratching my rear while my parents got married. (I was shocked!! What a mouth.)

Now, years later, we are still talking and laughing about the trip. We have flown the planes in several air shows, and they have been very well received. The Confederate Air Force Squadron of Missouri has taken us under their wings and let us mess around with the L-Birds at the air shows they fly in. You haven't lived until you have had two AT-6's roar by so close that you could hear their engines over your own. Sitting beside a Mustang while he is going through his mag checks can make you feel small and humble, too.

The plane is starting to catch on now. There are four Nieuports at our airport and we fly as often as we can. When the Dawn Patrol descends onto a "foreign" airport on one of our famous breakfast flights, action stops. It's the culmination of a long dream that started in 1985. Flying a warbird, even a cheap one, is a thrill not experienced by very many mortals. The opportunities for daydreaming are endless.

COMBAT!

I am not gracious in defeat.

We slowly and carefully stalked our unsuspecting prey. For thirty minutes we had ducked and dodged behind small gray clouds as we closed the distance. My sleek, deadly fighter quivered with suppressed excitement as we craftily worked our way up to our unsuspecting victim's six-o'clock low position. The lumbering Albatross C-1 droned on back to the German lines. The rear-facing observer, leaning against his machine gun, remained oblivious of the gray, shadowy, shark-like form flitting from cloud to shadowy cloud behind him.

The cratered, moonscape-like terrain of war-torn 1916 France slowly unrolled beneath us as I crept in closer and closer to my heedless quarry. We stealthily eased in behind him beneath his tail. I pulled the stick back and the nose of Le Faucon Gris rose to firing position. My steely blue eyes were narrowed to slits. My sensual lips curled in a disdainful sneer. My sinewy, muscular hands clutched the stick and throttle in a death grip. I was sure he couldn't hear the roar of the mighty Volkswagen 1700 over the tortured scream of his struggling Rotax 447. I centered his cockpit in my gun sight and gently caressed the trigger on my stick.

I blubbered my lips. "TOC-A-TOC-A-TOC-A-TOC-A," my deadly Lewis .303 machine gun mounted on the top wing of my canvas falcon bucked, shuddered and spat out a stream of death-dealing lead.

My sensual lips curled in a disdainful sneer.

I smiled grimly as a line of jagged bullet holes etched its deadly pattern along the fuselage of the Albatross. A burst of dirty smoke, a flicker of flame, and another dastardly foe of Democracy, Apple Pie, and the American Way of Life spun down into eternity, leaving a long streamer of smoke and flames. Victory was mine. I cautiously did a victorious aileron wiggle.

I fed in a little more throttle and pulled up beside Gary and Terry Poole in their Starflight XC-2000. They were enjoying another beautiful evening flight in their two-place ultralight, and both were smiling at the beauty of the silky smooth air and the breathtaking view we had of the Missouri River bottoms east of Kansas City. I smiled over at them, reached up and patted my Lewis gun, and indicated that I had shot them down without their even knowing what had happened.

Gary smiled at me in return and I could see him pull back the throttle. He slowed down and I forged ahead. Ah ha!! So he wanted to play slow flight challenge, did he? Well, two could play at this game. I eased my throttle lever back a bit, matched his move, and slowly dropped back to fly beside him again. I grinned smugly at him. The thrown gauntlet had been picked up! Terry had her camera out and was taking pictures of the battle.

Slow flight challenges are fun. Anybody can thrash along at full throttle and see who is the fastest. It takes a lot of concentration to mush along juggling throttle and stick to maintain altitude and go as slow as possible without stalling. It's a real effort to end up at full throttle, hanging on the prop, trying to stay just a few miles per hour above a stall while your opponent finally stalls and drops like a brick, leaving you in sole command of the skies.

My Nieuport 11 and I were masters of slow flight. I gleefully prepared to demolish another foolish challenger and watch him sink into the depths below. Gary slowed down, I slowed down. Air speed 40 mph. Gary slowed down some more and raised the nose of his plane to maintain altitude. I mirrored his every move. Air speed 35 mph. This is where my other opponents usually stalled and floundered down into the lower depths. What was this? He was still there! Then I watched with awe-struck eyes as he juggled power and controls and slowed down even more. I struggled to match this new speed. I had to add full power and hold a lot of back pressure to stay with him. Suddenly, I knew that I was going to lose this contest. Gary and Terry just sat there looking smug.

The needle of the airspeed indicator was flickering around the 30 mph mark as my Nieuport started its usual pre-stall shuddering and complaining. The rudder bar was shaking under my feet and the ailerons were loose and mushy. The airspeed indicator was just sinking below 30 mph indicated when she finally said, "To heck with this!" and dropped out of the sky. As I sank like a thrown anchor below the new slow-flight champion, I looked up just in time to see Gary, with a big, toothy smile on his face, wiggling his fingers at me in a cheery good-bye. I waved back at him with my famous finger salute that I reserve for the victors when I lose. I am not gracious in defeat. People love to beat me in anything just to see the childish scenes I throw.

I landed and waited for the post-flight BS to start. Gary and Terry taxied in. They got out of their plane and jauntily swaggered over to me. Gary poked me in the chest and sneered, "You can shoot me down with your wooden bullets, fly 30 miles per hour faster, climb faster and higher, sound better with your Volkswagen engine, but... You will never, never, ever be able to fly as slow as I can. Nyaaah! Nyaaah! Nyaaah!" A shout of laughter arose from the herd gathered around us.

I slunk back to my hangar to the sound of braying hoots from everyone there. There's nothing quite as odious as an obnoxious winner. The ashes of defeat were bitter in my mouth.

But I vowed I would return to fight another day.

* * *

As Dick Lemons and I taxied our Nieuport 11s out to the runway, we couldn't keep from grinning at each other. Since we had started flying together at Liberty Landing International Airport we had been competing in every way we could think of. Who could fly the slowest, the fastest, make the best wheel landings, prettiest chandelle etc., etc. Today we were going to try a little good old-fashioned combat. It should be interesting to see the contrast between his light Rotax-powered ultralight version of the Nieuport and my heavier Volkswagen-powered experimental version. He has me on climb, I have him on top speed. Neither by much. It should be interesting.

Dick took off first, leaving me in the usual cloud of dust from the gravel runway. I waited until he had started his crosswind turn to begin my takeoff roll. We had learned the hard way that you don't mess around with the unbelievable wake turbulence a Nieuport kicks up.

I shoved the throttle lever forward to the stop. We rocketed down the runway and lunged into the air in search of "The Hun in the Sun."

As I passed through 500 feet, I started to look for Dick. Aha! There he was, coming at me head-on, just a little bit higher than I was. I turned a little to the right to keep him on my left side and raised the nose of Le Faucon Gris to get to his altitude.

We flashed by each other and both immediately threw ourselves into hard left turns. We started circling, each trying to tighten our turns and get on the other's tail. As the turns got tighter, I had to cock my neck back further and further to keep him in sight. Soon we were both in 45-degree banked turns diametrically across from each other and pretty much holding our own trying to get on each other's tail. I could see straight down into his cockpit and he could see into mine. His bared teeth flashed in the sun across the 300 feet that separated us. (When you're only going 55 mph, you can make a really tight turn.) Sometimes he would gain on me and sometimes I would gain on him. It was a stalemate. Damn, this was fun! I was grinning so much my face hurt.

I could see now what the term "Lufberry Circle" meant in the aerial dogfights of WWI. In the under-powered, frail flying machines used in 1916, you usually won or lost in the first pass. If that didn't work, you just circled and circled, trying to get on the other guy's tail, and waited for him to make a mistake. Since the prevailing winds in France were usually from the west, the swirling combatants would slowly drift over the German lines. Sooner or later the Allied pilots would be forced by lack of fuel to break off the combat, dive away (hoping their wings stayed on), and try to make it back to the safety of their own lines.

Dick and I finally gave it up as a draw, practiced our formation flying for a while, and landed. We taxied in together, the Rotax and VW singing a weird symphony of power: TA-POCKATA RING-DING-DING TA-POCKATA RING DING-DING TA-POCKATA RING-DING-DING. As we taxied in, I started to daydream again. It is an art I have assiduously cultivated since I was a mere lad, dozing peacefully away in school. Dick and I aren't taxiing in at Liberty Landing Airport. We are in 1916 war-torn France... pilots in the famous

Lafayette Escadrille. We are returning from yet another dangerous, exhausting patrol in our deadly Nieuport 11s. Luxeuil, the village where the French children daily brought the Lafayette Escadrille's pilots flowers and croissants, is still unscathed. We have been keeping the hated and dreaded crimson Fokker E-III's, with their deadly synchronized Spandau machine guns, from strafing their homes.

As we throw the kill switch of our 80-horse Le Rhone rotary engines, smoke can still be seen wafting from the barrels of our machine guns. Our ruggedly handsome features, strained from brushes with fiery death, are streaked with stains from castor oil, gunsmoke, and exhaust. The tattered leather flying togs we wear reek with the stench of cordite, castor oil, and blood. We throw off our straps and wearily dismount from the cockpits of our deadly, faithful, bullet-riddled, war-weary steeds as crowds of beautiful, nubile, flaxen-haired, buxom, high-breasted, dewy-lipped, rosy-cheeked, French maidens look on with misty, passion-filled eyes and quivering thighs. (Cowabunga! Damn!! What a picture!!!)

As the prop shuddered to a stop, the sudden cessation of sound jerked me back to the present. It was just another quiet afternoon at Liberty Landing. Dick and I got out of our planes and looked at each other. He slowly started walking toward me, glaring daggers from his beady little eyes. I started toward him, my eyes slitted in hate. We were about a hundred feet apart. As we swaggered closer and closer to each other, I started to hum the theme from "High Noon." Our hands were hanging down by our hips, ready to grab our trusty shooting irons, and you could hear the jingle of our spurs. We met, grimly looked each other in the eye, and almost at the same time said to each other, "I WHUPPED YOUR BUTT!" Then we both collapsed in laughter.

The planes were put away and the grill was pulled out of the hangar and fired up. Folding chairs were set out and coolers of pop opened. As the hot dogs started to sizzle, the post-flight BS and insult session started its usual ebb and flow.

If there is any place more peaceful than a small airport at dusk, I don't know what it is. You couldn't find a more congenial group. This is what being a Sunday flyer is all about.

The Jury

The rail birds of doom strike again.

In the movie "Waldo Pepper," there is the big final scene where Waldo gets to fly simulated combat against Ernst Kessler, the famous German WWI ace. Waldo is in his Sopwith Camel and Kessler is in his deadly Fokker DR-1 triplane. After about five fantastic minutes of combat, Waldo and Kessler make head-on passes at each other. There is a collision and both seriously damage their planes. They end up flying alongside each other. Waldo and Kessler look over at each other, smile sadly, salute, and then each flies off to meet his destiny alone.

Waldo climbs up into the clouds and flies along with his landing gear dangling, broken from the collision. The camera zooms in on his face and you can see him looking around at the surrounding beauty. He sits there with this sad-happy expression on his face and gives a big heart-rending sigh. You suddenly realize that Waldo would like to stay right where he is forever but realizes that it is not to be. The CAA (predecessor to the FAA) is about to ground him permanently and end his flying career. He is broke. Flying is the only thing he loves. Waldo knows that once he lands, it is all over. The lonely piano music comes into the background and he flies into a cloud and disappears. End of picture.

I always get choked up at that point. As they say in that commercial, "It doesn't get any better than this." I've had that feeling several times in my little homebuilt Nieuport 11...

* * *

The wind swirling around the windshield was tugging at my cheeks and making my white silk scarf billow out behind me and occasionally drum on the tight fabric on the fuselage. The air was smooth and just cool enough. Le Faucon Gris and I were returning from another dangerous combat mission over the east Kansas City Missouri river bottoms. Countless marauding Fokker E-IIIs and menacing Gotha bombers had gone down in flames before my deadly Lewis .303 machine gun. I never even had to reload. We had also gone down low-level and strafed the trenches at Verdun on our way back from the raid on the German aerodrome located at Independence Memorial Airport. (That means we flew low-level over the soybean fields by the river.) All in all, it had been a most successful and gratifying flight.

My bird and I entered the right-hand pattern at the airport. The air was dead calm. The sun, low on the horizon, cast a pleasant, warm golden glow over the land. IT WAS JUST SWELL!! I was going to end up my flight like I usually did with about 15 minutes of touch-and-goes, just about the most enjoyable and pleasant recreational activity you can engage in without having to take your clothes off. Not near as tiring, either. (I guess I'm showing my age.)

I was in the middle of my downwind leg when I pulled the carburetor heat on and pulled the throttle lever by my left side back to 2000 rpm. The mighty 1700cc Volkswagen ceased its fierce bellowing and settled down to a happy mutter. The oil temperature started down and the slow-turning prop was shimmering in the late afternoon sun. Life was full and complete!!

As I turned from base to final I took one last look around, as I always do, to make sure nobody had sneaked into the pattern on me. I glanced over to the line of hangars and suddenly my hand gripped the stick convulsively, my heart started to pound and my cheeks sucked in. Oh, for gawdsake! The Jury was out!! About five of the rail birds were sitting out there lined up in their lawn chairs waiting for me to land. They reminded me of a flock of hungry vultures sitting on a power line.

Suddenly the perfect afternoon flight turned brown and the fun went out of the evening. Drat! Nothing can screw up a landing as quickly as knowing that even one person is watching and evaluating.

Now, to make it worse, we have The Jury. The Liberty Landing International Airport evaluation judges were on duty. Geeze! Talk about pressure!!!

Let me tell you about The Jury.

Since Tom and I had moved our Nieuports out to Liberty Landing International, some changes had come into our lives. You remember the time I stood Tweety on her nose? Then you know what I mean about the crowd. The gang at Noah's was all male: sweaty and profane. Conversation was blunt, couched in scatological terms, and to the point. Now we always have the ladies present and have been forced to clean up our act a bit. (Ha! We've had to clean it up a *lot*.) The ladies are just as caustic and sarcastic as the men when commenting on a lousy landing, although their cutting language is just a tad bit more civilized. In fact, now that I think of it, the women are harder to please on landings than the men.

Anyway, we were all sitting out in front of the hangars one night, watching a student pilot shooting touch-and-goes, when the idea was brought up about forming a jury to judge and evaluate landings. We decided to score landings on the Liberty Landing International Airport five point system. It is the following:

Five: Fantabulous!! The best I've ever seen. I couldn't do better myself. You are a master pilot.

Four: Very good!! I've seen better, I just can't remember where.

Three: Average. I could do that good with my eyes closed.

Two: Nice bounces. Are you going to log them all?

One: The basic squat-and-leave-it. You're lucky you were able to taxi in. You'd better check your plane to see if anything fell off.

Zero: Go get the trailer, boys!!

It was Terry Poole's idea that we get numbered signs and display them like the judges do at the Olympics. I have never seen that woman make a bad landing or even bounce her Starflight XC-2000. She doesn't have to worry; the thing will land in 20 feet if there is a headwind coming down the runway.

Now here I was on short final. I could practically see the judges licking their lips in anticipation of my landing. I carefully lined Le Faucon Gris up on the center of the runway and pulled the throttle back to idle. We crossed over the threshold, the flying wires whistling their weird discordant symphony in the wind. I could sense The Jury watching intently as I eased the stick back to start the flare. The tailwheel touched just an instant before the mains brushed the gravel. NO BOUNCES! IT WAS A GREASER!! PRAISE THE LORD!!! I was pleased. We turned off the runway and started to waddle back to the hangar. I saw the jury comparing notes and choosing their numbered cards. As I turned the corner all the cards went up and I could see the scores. Hmmmmmmm. Three 4s, a 5 (from Sharon, bless her heart), a 3 (my brother-in-law; he doesn't know anything), and a 2 (Dick Lemons is jealous). All in all, not a bad score from this band of gimlet-eyed crooks.

I quickly shut the bird down, jumped out, grabbed my score cards and joined the happy, chattering band waiting for their next victim to enter the pattern. Seeing that motley crew lined up in their easy chairs when you are on short final guarantees you that any good landing you make that day is going to have been made under the most trying circumstances you will ever encounter while flying. As usual, at our airport, IT'S AN ABSOLUTE BALL! Every evening the landing competitions go on, and as a result, all you do is get better, and that's what recreational flying is all about.

Truly, I feel sorry for pilots who have to fly out of big airports and don't get the opportunity to get into the activities of a small, intimate, short-runway, no-tower, we-are-flying-for-the-fun-of-it airport. Usually, air traffic controllers are too busy to comment on your landings.

You just know that somewhere out there, the perfect landing is just waiting for you to make it. If (when) you finally do make it, then you know that there is an even better one waiting out there and you start to strive for it. It's a never-ending and enormously pleasurable activity. You hone and enhance your flying skills while having more fun than should be legally possible.

A New Bird

And some new surprises.

It was finally done! Complete! Finished! Nothing else to do. Painted, engine test run, controls calibrated and tweaked. My new Kolb Twinstar Mark II sat there in the back yard quivering with excitement like it couldn't wait to jump into the air and fly. Ready in every way — or so I thought.

It had taken me two and a half years of off-and-on work to finish her, but it was worth it. Any decent mechanic could have done it in one fourth the time, but I didn't care. This plane was mine. When Tom Glaeser and I built our Nieuport 11s, it had been a different story: I hadn't done a lot of the design work or heavy thought on the Nieuports. I had been more of an apprentice in the workshop doing what Tom told me to do.

This time it was different. Even though I had bought the "quick build" option with my kit, I had done it all myself. Every rivet, every hole drilled, every run in the paint, every hole punched into the unpainted fabric. I had done them all, and was I proud! She looked good too: all white with red and blue sunburst trim — a garish celebration of flight.

It had all started when I finally had to bite the bullet and sell the Tweety Bird. We had experienced many beautiful and magic moments together but several factors forced me to put her on the market. One:

the completion of my Nieuport 11 fighter—more fun to fly than anything I could think of, and two: the passage of Rule 88-2, the "transponder with Mode C" rule. Rule 88-2 basically ended Tweety Bird's stay at Noah's Ark International Airport, because Noah's is located right on the edge of the Kansas City International Airport TCA's inner ring. Every plane owner there was scrambling to get transponders with Mode C altitude encoders installed, moving their planes, or in extreme cases like mine, putting them up for sale.

I got two quotes on getting a transponder installed in Tweety and both times, the transponder was the minor expense. Her electrical system could not handle any more load, and further inspection showed that to comply with the new regulations would have necessitated a complete electrical system removal and replacement. So, with bitter thoughts and tear-filled eyes, I watched her disappear into the distance, heading to her new home in the boondocks of Southern Missouri. I knew she'd be happy down there far away from TCAs and ARSAs. (Ironically, Rule 88-2 was later "reinterpreted" by the FAA to allow exemptions to planes with marginal or no electrical systems.)

Two weeks later, I visited the Kolb company and took a ride in the Mark II they used for demos. Besides being a sweetheart in the air, this two-place ultralight has unbelievable visibility, with a large wrap-around windshield that allows it to be flown in cold weather. Another thing that really decided me to go with the Kolb Twinstar was the option of having the quick-build kit. Since I don't have a basement or even a whole garage to work in, a quick-build kit would enable me to cut as many corners as I legally could and still get a plane that I could build myself. Well, it worked.

I had already gone through the FAA paperwork that I thought was required. They had my letter of intent. I had visited the FSDO and let an inspector go over the plans and tell me if there was anything he didn't like in them.

As the plane got closer and closer to completion, my fever got hotter and hotter. The white paint was applied. Then the red trim. Then the blue. The Rotax 503 engine was mounted and run to see if all the instruments worked. They did. All the required placards and markings were applied in their appropriate locations. She was ready. At least I thought she was.

I called the FAA office and made an appointment to get the final inspection appointment in a week. I needed to get the wings and tail mounted and all control cables safety wired and checked over, and planned this for Saturday. Up to that point, it had been a pretty mild winter—Friday night, we got a four-inch snowfall.

This presented a problem. Those wings had to be mounted. Tricia was still away at Missouri University. My dad isn't limber enough to do it. So, in desperation, I turned to my soul mate, my sweetie-pie, my partner in life, Sharon. From 25 years of marriage, I knew the perfect bait.

"Sweetie," I said with my biggest disarming smile, "If you'll help me put the wings on the plane today, I'll take you out to dinner at a restaurant."

Sharon turned to me, her eyes wide open with awe and incredulous amazement. "You mean a sit down place with a waiter and everything?"

"Yep," I said. "We're going to go all out for this one." With a big smile she ran to get her grubby clothes on and the trial by fire—and ice—was ready to begin.

That's how it happened that Sharon and I spent all day Saturday rolling around in the soggy wet snow in the back yard, frantically putting in clevis pins, cotter pins in castle nuts, safety wiring turnbuckles and all the other assorted little goodies that are a real thrill to do with numb fingers. The dinner that night at Denny's was a real festive occasion.

With that daunting little task behind me, it was time to call in the big guns to look her over. First I asked my long-suffering buddy Tom to come over and give her a final look-see before The Man showed up.

Tom strolled into the back yard where the Kolb was waiting in her patch of trampled snow. He walked up to the front and stood there with his hands in his pockets whistling quietly through his teeth. Then, with a disgusted look on his face, he started to walk away, saying, "Call me again when she's *really* ready."

"What do you mean?" I yelled. "This plane is done. It's ready."

Tom gave me a pitying look. "Standing right here, I can see two bolts with no nuts on them, two bolts with the nuts only started, and a castle nut with no cotter pin in it."

I looked where he was pointing on the landing gear legs. Rats! He was right. How did I miss those? Tom roared off and I started from the rear of that plane and began looking at every nut, bolt, rivet, and everything else I could think of. I found a lot. I just couldn't see how I had missed those. Tom came back, and this time it took him a lot longer to find a few minor squawks, and they were easily fixed. Then I called old Eagle-Eye.

My dad got his A & P in 1937 and grew up in the golden age of aviation. He is an expert on the old piston engines and retired as a power plant engineer specializing in the PRT — Power Recovery Turbine — or, as it was also referred to, the Parts Recovery Trap, on the Wright Cyclone R-3350. His reputation as a beady-eyed, hard-headed, suspicious, super-picky mechanic is nation-wide.

Dad arrived with a flashlight, a little mechanic's mirror on a probe, and assorted other little tools of his trade. He started his inspection at the nose and began to progress down the port side. I quickly got my clipboard and started making notes of the comments, snide remarks, bursts of rage, and exclamations of disgust that followed his progress around the plane.

"Torque this nut some more. Spray this ball and socket with some LPS-3. Redo this safety wire on this turnbuckle. Clean this, clean that! Blah fix blah re-do blah-de-blah tighten more blah re-do this blah replace this blah."

I was starting my second page of notes when he got to the tailwheel. He grunted as he got down on his hands and knees in the snow and crawled under the horizontal stabilizer.

There were assorted mutterings and exclamations that were suddenly ended by a scream of rage.

"AAUGGH!" he cried. "WHAT THE HELL IS THIS??!!" He shot out from under the tail in a shower of snow and thrust an index finger under my nose. His outraged face was crimson and his jowls were quivering.

"LOOK AT THAT!" he roared. "JUST LOOK AT THAT!"

There was a little, itty-bitty, teensie-weensie spot of blood on his finger. He'd cut himself on something.

Gulp! I gave him a sickly smile. "Heh heh heh... I must have missed something down there."

"NO BLANK!!" He'd reached the hissing stage by then. "I got this off the blankety cotter pin on the blankety tail blank wheel blank swivel bolt." He threw in a few more blanks as he sucked on his punctured finger and got his breath. He was gathering steam now. "I SHOULD BE ABLE TO RUN MY FINGER OVER ANY BOLT ON THIS PLANE AND NEVER FIND A SHARP EDGE. AND I WILL!" he roared.

The bottom line was that before he left, every cotter pin in every castle nut on the plane had been replaced, clipped and bent to his satisfaction. It was worth it all, though. By the time he left, she was *ready*! And with two days to spare, too.

Now was the time to do one more check on the most difficult part of getting an experimental aircraft certified: the paperwork. I hate this part.

I got out my registration form, weight and balance, equipment list, engine and aircraft logbooks, builder's log, plans, and a photo album of the plane's building progress. They were all laid out on the dining room table and ready to be examined.

On Monday, Mr. Larry Becherer, the inspector from FSDO #63, showed up. He arrived with a large briefcase full of official-looking papers and a small portable typewriter. He also had all the same kinds of tools and inspection equipment that my dad had brought over.

An unexpected person arrived, too. Glenn Huff is an ex-WWII Sea Bee and was building a Nieuport 12. He has been picking my brains about covering, paint, rivets and all the other little items involved with building a tube and gusset, fabric-covered plane.

He is also one hell of a practical joker and I cringed when he showed up. I knew he was just waiting for the perfect time to strike.

The first thing Larry wanted to see was my assorted paperwork.

The plans were examined first, and while dad and Glenn traded stories about life in the '40s and '50s, Larry silently pored over page after page of the plans. I stood there on one foot then the other, wondering what he was going to find fault with first. He studied the plans for an hour, and asked me for several clarifications on how I had followed certain procedures detailed in the plans and instruction manual. I was able to answer all his questions by referring to my photo album and the notes in my builder's log.

He finished the plans and started to go through the rest of the paperwork. The weight and balance... no problem. My equipment list... again, no problem.

Things were going great!! Then the hammer of Thor descended.

Larry turned to me and started asking for some paperwork I had never heard of. It was then that I learned that things had changed since Tom and I had certified the Nieuports back in 1986.

The first form he wanted was Advisory Circular AC No. 20-27D "Certification and Operation of Amateur-Built Aircraft."

I didn't have it.

Then he asked me for my form 8130-6, the application for an airworthiness certificate.

I didn't have that, either.

My dad was looking pretty disgusted by now, and Glenn was having trouble holding back his snickers.

Larry looked at me and sighed. "Do you have your notarized form 8130-12, Eligibility Statement — Amateur-Built Aircraft?"

GULP. "No."

Larry sighed. Dad looked more disgusted. Glenn grinned.

"Do you have your aircraft and engine logbooks?"

Well, now! Things were looking better. These I had. He spent about twenty minutes going over the logs and pointing out things I needed to fix and/or do over. He also gave me copies of the missing papers and told me to have them completed when he came out to the airport to give her the final once-over.

I was feeling pretty bad by now, but Larry just grinned and said, "I'm going to have to do a final inspection when you get your plane out to the airport. You can have all your other paperwork done by then and I'll sign it off." He grinned and rubbed his hands together. "Now, let's go look at the plane."

We went out into the snow-covered back yard. He started his inspection with the pitot tube and proceeded to look at every single instrument connection, hose, hose clamp, rivet, nut, bolt, screw, cable swedge, turnbuckle, joint, hinge, and connection on that plane.

He was as picky as my dad, but not as sarcastic. I followed him with my ever-present clipboard, making notes of the things he wanted fixed or added.

Glenn went into high gear — this was what he had been waiting for. As we all followed Larry around the plane, Glenn kept up a running patter as he pointed to different parts of the plane. "Are you going to let him get away with this?" or "Burke, is this where you made him fix that real big screw-up he was telling me about?"

The inspection proceeded in spite of Glenn's help. Larry finally got back to his starting point, and we gathered around to discuss the list. Thankfully, it was short, sweet and simple: Add white, green, yellow, and red arcs to the airspeed indicator, add "off" and "on" labels to the strobe light switch, add a compass card and holder to the compass, and replace the cotter pin on the elevator mechanism castle nut. (Dad had told me to fix it and I forgot. I'm still shuddering from the look he gave me when Larry brought it to our attention.)

Aside from the debacle over the paperwork, the project had come out pretty well. I ordered the airspeed arcs and compass card from Aircraft Spruce and Specialty, and got the necessary paperwork completed during the rest of the week.

We trailered the plane out to the airport, where she was unloaded and the wings were attached. Before I could taxi-test her up and down our little 1800-foot runway, I had to go through the ritual of breaking in the Rotax engine.

You can break in a Rotax engine in only one hour. One very long, noisy hour. Five minutes at 3500 rpm, one minute at 5000 rpm, one minute at 2000 rpm, five minutes at 4000 rpm, one minute at 5500 rpm, one minute at 2000 rpm, five minutes at 4500 rpm, ten seconds at full throttle (6000–6200 rpm), one minute at 2000 rpm, five minutes at 5000 rpm, fifteen seconds at full throttle, one minute at 2000 rpm, five minutes at 5000 rpm, twenty seconds at full throttle, one minute at 2000 rpm, five minutes at 5000 rpm, thirty seconds at full throttle, one minute at 2000 rpm, five minutes at 5500 rpm, five minutes at 4000 rpm, one minute at full throttle, one minute at 2000 rpm, two minutes at full throttle, one minute at 2000 rpm, five minutes at 5500 rpm, and finally—thankfully—two minutes at full throttle.

I had to be led from the plane like a zombie. Although I was wearing hearing protectors, I was still deaf and shaking from the screaming of the two-cycle engine. I was used to the calm mutter of the Volkswagen at idle and the comfortable roar of it at a 2700-rpm cruise. Now, here I was running an engine that *idled* at a speed only a little slower than what I was used to cruising at. What's worse, every time you put new rings in the Rotax, a fairly regular operation, you have to go through it again. I couldn't wait.

The engine was now ready to go, so I taxi-tested her for three hours on the runway getting the feel of her. Up and down, up and down. She

I had to be led from the plane like a zombie.

handled a lot different from the short-coupled little Nieuport — much more docile and not quite as twitchy. I stood her on her nose only once while testing the brakes. I knew then why the Kolb has that skid on the nose. Works good, too! The taxi-testing went on and on. Slow, fast, tail high, tail low, swerving, straight, I got used to how she handled on the ground. The Kolb is so low that I got the feeling I was on a 100-mph go-kart.

Larry Becherer came out to the airport for the final inspection. I was ready. I had paperwork coming out my ears, and all the items he mentioned in his first inspection had been fixed. He spent about thirty minutes going over the plane and then asked for an engine run-up. It went great. No squawks. The final papers were signed off and she was done, certified, legal!

It was too bad that the wind was gusting ninety degrees to the runway. I decided to make the first flight on a calm day with no crowd. I'd seen too many pilots mess up a brand new plane by being pressured into making their first flight on a totally unsuitable day.

A few days later, that first flight was a pure joy. The hours of slow taxi-testing paid off, and fifteen seconds after a trouble-free lift-off I had her trimmed to hands-off cruise. She is a real sweetheart to fly... very positive response to control inputs... no bad habits. As I write this, I am flying off the required 40 hours in my flight test area. And I am looking forward to the time when I can take my first passengers up and share the joy of flight in my new bird.

The Wife

Do you know yours?

As you read through the preceding pages, it is quite possible that you might have come across a few slight, tiny exaggerations about my life with Sharon, my continually suffering wife. She is, deservedly, an object of pity with many of the women in the neighborhood. I will leave it up to you to decide which recollections are the truth and which are fabrications.

The one thing I didn't exaggerate was my description of Sharon when she is aggravated. An enraged, red-faced Sharon in full cry with fangs bared and quivering talons outstretched is an awesome apparition that no sane or sober individual will purposely cross. Just ask her students.

But I do feel just a little bit guilty about some of the other things you have read about her. I like to pretend that I am a henpecked, constantly suffering husband, but the exact opposite is true. Sharon has never been anything but outstandingly supportive of all my hobbies and recreational pursuits. She knows I will never be anything but a 14-year-old in my heart and mind. I know that a lot of my male acquaintances are jealous of the relationship Sharon and I have. I thank my lucky stars every time I think about her. Not many wives would put up with what she has gone through.

For example, I was thumbing through a flying magazine a few days back and I saw an ad in the classified section that possessed a certain familiarity:

> FOR SALE: Sky-blazer 150 project. Fuselage on gear. All instruments, engine, covering material, many extras, over $15,000 and five years invested. Wife says it's got to go, will take best offer. Call 555-5555.

I had seen ads just like it many times before. If you look behind the lines, you can read a very sad story. Many a marriage has gone through some trying times because of the "homebuilt airplane disease." Constructing a homebuilt airplane takes a dedication and commitment between husband and wife that's rarely found in other recreational pursuits.

For any married man thinking about learning to fly, the reaction the wife will have to this expensive new madness has to be carefully considered. I hope you are as lucky in your choosing of a mate as I have been. Some wives are reluctant to face the long hours of loneliness associated with a spouse's fanatical pursuit of that special dream plane. They also bitterly resent the constant leakage the check book experiences.

And when you figure that some homebuilt aircraft take five to ten years to build, you can see why an understanding wife is a vital necessity for any man interested in building a plane.

So if you finally do decide to "Slip the surly bonds of earth" and enter this wonderful, rewarding activity, try to gauge your wife's feelings about it first while you are telling her how important this will be to you. You might be surprised at how supportive and interested she will be. (Of course, she might cut you off at the knees, too. Try to make a very good guess before you leap.)

While we're on the subject, I saw another ad that you might find enlightening:

> FOR SALE: Award-winning Cowabunga, 100 hours, new paint, excellent interior, flies like a dream. Cruises at 260 mps, lands at 55, full IFR panel, over $30,000 and eight years invested. Wife says it's got to go. Will take best offer. On second thought, make offer on wife. Call for photo, measurements, and personality details, 555-5555.

Kinda says it all, doesn't it?

A Glossary of Useful Aviation Terms

And a few that aren't.

A & P (Airframe & Powerplant) A mechanic, licensed by the FAA, who can make repairs to aircraft. A very nice person to make friends with. A little major-class groveling might be in order.

AD (Airworthiness Directive) A non-negotiable command from the FAA to fix, usually at your own expense, something incredibly expensive on your plane or engine that has caused problems on other aircraft of the same model. Unexpected ADs have severely dented a lot of pocketbooks and even more marriages.

ADF (Automatic Direction Finder) A real neat little instrument to have. With this in your aircraft, you can tune in the local AM radio station and the ADF needle will lead you right to the town as you listen to your favorite country western tunes.

AGL The height of the aircraft Above the Ground Level. Since the ground has its ups and downs, this measurement is not indicated by the altimeter unless the ground below you happens to be at sea level. If your altimeter reads 4800 feet and you're flying by Denver, you're about 400 feet underground.

AILERON The movable control surface on the wing that makes the plane bank to the right and left. The ailerons control movement about the longitudinal (roll) axis of the aircraft.

ALTIMETER The instrument that indicates the height of the

aircraft above sea level. Air traffic controllers will give you the altimeter setting (barometric pressure) so you can adjust your altimeter to give an accurate reading.

AMMETER The instrument that apprises you of the charging status of your aircraft's electrical system.

AOPA Aircraft Owners and Pilots Association. This organization monitors the pulse of aviation and lobbies strongly for pilots' rights in Washington. Membership entitles you to receive a monthly magazine that will keep you abreast of aviation news. A useful organization to belong to.

ARTIFICIAL HORIZON This instrument (also called an attitude indicator) will tell you the relative position of your aircraft — with respect to pitch and roll — with the horizon. It is probably the most important instrument used in instrument flying. Flying on instruments without an artificial horizon is a nerve-wracking experience.

ATA (Airport Traffic Area) The regulated airspace, with a five-mile radius and a height of 3500 feet, that surrounds a tower-controlled airport. Inbound, you are supposed to contact the tower before entering the ATA. The controllers tend to get cranky if you call in after you have landed and request taxi instructions.

BASE LEG The course in an airport traffic pattern at a 90 degree-angle to the final approach course.

CARBURETOR HEAT The venturi effect of air entering the throat of an airplane engine's carburetor allows ice to form under certain climate conditions and power settings. If enough ice accumulates, the engine will quit due to fuel starvation. This usually happens on landing approach, the worst time. The carburetor heat system directs air that has been warmed by the engine to the carburetor to prevent icing or to melt any ice that has been formed.

CFI (Certified Flight Instructor) An individual who is licensed by the FAA to give flight instruction.

CG (CENTER OF GRAVITY) The measured point on an airplane at which it would balance if it were suspended. This measurement is very important, since having a CG too far to the rear or too far forward could make the plane unmanageable. Every aircraft must have on board a weight and balance data sheet stating the allowable CG limits, fore and aft. The pilot must load the plane with fuel, people, and baggage in such a way as to stay within the CG "envelope."

CHECKLIST A list that helps the pilot to remember to perform all the required inspections and procedures. There is a Before Start checklist, Engine Start checklist, Engine Warm-up checklist, Before Takeoff checklist, Before Landing checklist, and Putting the Plane Away checklist.

CHECK RIDE These are a necessary evil. You must take a check ride with an FAA certified flight examiner to obtain your pilot certificate, and then undergo a *biennial flight review* every two years. Check rides are usually in two parts, the oral and the flight. During the oral, the examiner will question you about rules, chart reading, weight and balance, and anything else he wants to. During the flight portion of the ride, s/he will evaluate your in-flight performance and test you for hooded instrument flight, unusual attitudes, stalls, landings and simulated (you hope) emergencies.

COMPASS VARIATION See MAGNETIC VARIATION.

CONCRETE COMPASS This is called flying IFIS. (I Fly Inter-States.) A Rand-McNally map is helpful, but you need an aeronautical chart to know where the airports, obstructions, and "keep out" areas are located.

CROSS COUNTRY You must have 10 hours, minimum, of cross-country flying to obtain a private pilot's license. Your first one will be a dual cross-country flight with your flight instructor. If you are able to satisfy the flight instructor that you can be trusted to find your destination airport and get back, he or she will sign you off for your solo cross-country flights. As far as I am concerned, any flight where you don't land at the same place you took off from is a cross-country flight.

CROSSWIND TURN The first turn an aircraft makes after takeoff, usually a 90-degree turn away from the runway.

DARK-THIRTY The time, usually very early in the morning, when everybody with a lick of sense, except pilots, is still in bed. Morning, especially during the summer, is the best time to fly. The air is usually cool and smooth. Later on, when the temperature starts to rise and the thermals begin to pop, the air can sometimes be as rough as driving a car, full speed, across a freshly plowed field.

DEVIATION The behavior of a weird person. Also, the error found in a magnetic compass caused by the attraction of various ferrous metals in the plane. All planes have a compass deviation card by the compass which informs the pilot of the degrees of error in the compass at different headings.

DG (Directional Gyro) See GYRO COMPASS.

DME (Distance Measuring Equipment) If you are lucky enough to have one in your aircraft, this radio will tell you how far, in miles, you are from a particular VOR station. It will also display your groundspeed and the time required to get to the station.

DOWNWIND LEG The course followed by a plane, parallel with the active runway, when going downwind (opposite the landing direction) in the traffic pattern at an airport.

EAA (Experimental Aircraft Association) Probably the best organization to join if you are planning on building your own aircraft or even if you are just interested in planes. There are EAA chapters scattered all over the country, and the members will be able to give you building tips as well as advise you of aircraft for sale and which flight instructors to approach about learning to fly.

ELEVATORS The movable control surfaces back at the tail, attached to the horizontal stabilizer, that adjust the pitch of the aircraft. The aircraft will rotate around its CG, or center of gravity, when the elevators are moved up or down, normally causing the plane to go up or down in flight. See also CG.

ELT (Emergency Locator Transmitter) An expensive little piece of hardware that is supposed to automatically activate itself if you have an accident. The ELT has a reputation for not working when it needs to and turning itself on when it shouldn't. It transmits a steady signal on 121.5 megahertz, the emergency channel. Theoretically, the searchers will be able to find where you went down by following the radio signals. A friend of mine put his in the trunk of his car. He hit a pothole on the way home from the airport and activated it. Several hours later a helicopter was circling his house and police cars were at his door. There was a lot of excitement. Another friend stood his plane on its nose when his brakes locked up and the ELT did not activate itself. ELTs seem to have a failure rate of about 50%.

ETA (Estimated Time of Arrival) This is when you hope you will get there (*if* you don't get lost).

FAA (Federal Aviation Administration) The guys you don't want to mess with. The Big Brother of the air. If they say "Jump," you say "How high?"

FARs (Federal Air Regulations)   Rules for flight. If you break one, you will be contacted by some very unpleasant individuals (see FAA).

FBO (Fixed Base Operator)   The individual or company, located at an airport, that will sell gas, clean and repair aircraft and engines, and arrange for tiedown or hangar space. Many operate flight schools as well.

FINAL APPROACH   The path followed by the plane when it finally lines up with the runway it is planning to land on. For small aircraft landing at small airports, final approaches are rarely longer than a mile and often much shorter. For Nieuports at a small airport, final approach is usually about 300 feet.

FLAPS   The movable control surfaces, attached to the trailing edges of the wings, that allow the pilot to adjust the camber of the wings at low speeds. This added camber creates more lift and drag and allows the aircraft to take off and land at lower airspeeds. Flaps also allow a much steeper descent without increasing the airspeed. If your aircraft doesn't have flaps, you have to learn to side slip. (See SLIP.)

FLARE   The final maneuver made by the aircraft while landing. The descent of the aircraft is checked and the plane is stalled onto the ground at a carefully calculated altitude, hopefully only a few inches. Student pilots have been known to flare from heights ranging from five feet to minus five feet.

FLIGHT PLAN   This is a little form you can fill out over the phone, or over the radio, or in person at a FSS. It tells the FAA where you are going, the altitude you are going to try to fly at, and when you are expected to get there. If you don't show up, they go looking for you. Flight plans offer a little feeling of security. You should file one before going on any long cross-country.

FSDO (Flight Standards District Office)   One of the bureaucratic arms of the FAA that police general aviation and the airlines. These individuals are the ones who will inspect homebuilt aircraft and also drop the hammer on you if you break an FAR. You don't want to get on their bad side.

FSS (Flight Service Station)   These are usually located at airports, and pilots can receive weather briefings and file flight plans there. The Flight Service Specialists are usually polite and helpful.

FUSELAGE   The body of the plane that the wings and tail

feathers are attached to. Usually covered, sometimes open framework.

GLIDE Flight without power. Gravity is your only motive force. This is fun only when you do it on purpose. If the engine quits, your plane becomes a glider. You have to come down, but you are still able to control it and will probably make a safe landing – if you don't panic.

GLOBAL POSITIONING SYSTEM (GPS) A navigation system that uses signals sent by satellites to provide very precise position information. Most GPS receivers can give you your ground speed, estimated time of arrival, nearest airport, warnings when you're approaching a TCA or other restricted airspace, and a whole plethora of other stuff that you just might need. There are even handheld sets that can be moved from plane to plane.

GROUND LOOP The most exciting carnival ride known to man. This maneuver results when you lose directional control while on the ground. It usually happens to a tailwheel-equipped aircraft during a crosswind landing. The plane rotates around its vertical axis and sometimes digs in a wing tip. The old rule of thumb is that "There are those taildragger pilots who have ground looped and those who are going to." But like many rules of thumb, "It ain't necessarily so."

GROUND SCHOOL Every prospective pilot must pass two different tests to get his license: a flight check ride with an FAA authorized check pilot, and a (gasp, shudder) written test. The Private Pilot's written test covers every aspect of flying from soup to nuts: radio procedures, air space rules, navigation, weather, instruments – you name it. If it concerns a plane or flying, they're gonna test you on it. You learn all this stuff in ground school. I did my ground school on my own with study guides; you can also buy videotaped courses. Another alternative is to go to your friendly airport flying school and take your ground school instruction there. Some schools will even do the whole ball of wax on a single weekend, but there is some controversy as to whether these cram courses teach you what you really ought to know or just get you through the test.

GYRO COMPASS Sometimes called the directional gyro. This instrument is used in conjunction with the magnetic compass in the aircraft. A small, rapidly spinning wheel, coupled with an indicator, will give you a very steady display of your direction of flight. Gyro compasses do not jump around and spin like magnetic compasses.

They do have to be checked every 15 minutes or so to see if they need to be manually reset to match the magnetic compass.

HOOD (INSTRUMENT) A fiendish tool designed to torture student pilots. It is like a baseball hat with a large, contoured visor. When wearing a hood, the victim can't see anything except the instrument panel. This is used to train for flying solely by reference to instruments. Trying to peek out from under the hood (to see how you're doing) will usually get you a nasty shot in the ribs from your instructor.

HORIZONTAL STABILIZER This horizontally mounted, non-moving control surface is what the elevators attach to. It adds pitch stability to the plane in flight. On some aircraft, the entire horizontal tail surface moves. In that configuration, it is called a stabilator.

IA (Inspection Authorization) MECHANIC A licensed mechanic who can inspect and approve repairs to aircraft. Another individual to make friends with.

IFR (Instrument Flight Rules) Regulations affecting flight under instrument conditions, where you often can't see where you're going. If you are not instrument rated, you don't want to fly in these conditions. Once I saw a sign in a Flight Service Station that said, "Having an instrument rating means you should know enough not to go in the first place." Usually, if a light aircraft is equipped with an IFR panel, there is more money tied up in the radios and instruments than in the plane itself.

IRON COMPASS The same as the concrete compass except you follow railroad tracks instead of roads. This is called flying IFRR. (I follow rail roads.) It's easy to do. A sectional map shows railroads in detail and just about any small town has tracks leading to it. If you ever get really lost and find some railroad tracks, follow them to the next town. Then you should be able to find it on the sectional map and go on from there.

JET WASH See WAKE TURBULENCE.

LORAN Long Range Navigation system using chains of transmitters that computes position information that is almost as precise as GPS. Loran receivers are low in cost and provide information similar to the GPS sets.

MAGNETIC COMPASS An aircraft magnetic compass, usually suspended in a non-freezing liquid. It is very difficult to read in bumpy air. If you are going to be doing a lot of long cross-country work, a gyro compass is a definite must.

MAGNETIC VARIATION (COMPASS VARIATION) The difference in degrees, determined by your location, between true north and magnetic north (where your compass points). When flying by *dead reckoning*, without using radionavigation, you must compensate for magnetic variation.

MAGNETO The primary source of ignition in almost all aircraft. A magneto is an entirely self-contained ignition system and does not depend on any outside components like batteries or coils to operate. Most aircraft possess two magnetos, which give two totally independent ignition systems.

MEDICAL CERTIFICATE Every licensed pilot must pass a flight physical. There are three classes of medical certificates: First, Second, and Third. A private pilot only has to have a Third Class, the least restrictive and easiest to get. For a Third Class, you must be "inspected" every two years. It's no big deal.

MODE C See TRANSPONDER.

MSL The height of the aircraft above Mean Sea Level, not above the ground. See also ALTIMETER; AGL.

NOTAMS (Notices to Airmen) These notices, disseminated by Flight Service Stations, notify you of any important changes in procedures or facilities concerning airspace and airports you are planning to use.

OIL PRESSURE The oil pressure gauge tells you a lot about the health of your engine. If the pressure starts to fall, you need to think about landing soon!

OIL TEMPERATURE This instrument is also very important in evaluating the health of your engine. If the temperature starts to rise, you need to land soon. If oil pressure starts to fall and oil temperature goes up at the same time, you really need to look for a landing place *right now.*

PANIC BUTTON This is what you push when you run out of options. It is usually associated with a high, squeaky voice on the radio.

PATTERN The standard flight path used by aircraft during takeoff and landing procedures.

PITOT TUBE A small tube, usually located on the leading edge of the wing of a light aircraft. Air pressure from the aircraft's passage through the air acts on a very sensitive instrument that indicates your speed through the air. This is usually different from groundspeed, which is affected by winds.

PREFLIGHT INSPECTION This is what you do before even untieing the plane. The aircraft is given a complete walk-around inspection, including fuel, oil, control surfaces, landing gear, etc.

PROPPING   Starting the engine by manually swinging the propeller through the compression stroke. Not fun and potentially dangerous. It should be attempted only by someone who knows what he is doing.

PUCKER FACTOR A physiological reaction to stress while in an aircraft. It is commonly measured on a scale from one to ten, dependent on the grip your rear end gets on the seat cushion of the aircraft. One, the lowest rating on the scale, is usually caused by a missed beat in the engine or being lost for five or less minutes. Ten, the highest, results from sudden engine failures at night or ground loops. A Ten-Plus reading is reserved for a call from the FAA saying they are here to help and would like to have a talk with you.

RUDDER The movable vertical control surface, attached to the vertical fin, used in conjunction with the ailerons to make it possible for the aircraft to make a "coordinated turn" (no skidding). The rudder controls movement about the vertical axis (yaw) of the aircraft. The rudder is usually also connected with either the tailwheel or nosewheel for directional control on the ground.

RUNWAY NUMBERING This indicates the direction the runway faces based on magnetic compass headings rounded off to the nearest ten degrees. Each runway has two numbers. Example: Runway 9-27 faces 090 degrees and 270 degrees, depending on whether you are landing to the east (runway 9) or landing to the west (runway 27). Usually, the numbers are painted at the end of the runway in very large letters.

SECTIONAL CHART Your basic VFR navigational chart. You can buy them at any airport. Sectional charts are updated every six months and you are required to have current charts for the areas in which you fly.

SLIP A side slip or forward slip is used primarily in aircraft without flaps to lose altitude rapidly without gaining excess airspeed. On an approach to landing, a side slip is initiated to compensate for a crosswind and a forward slip is used when there is no crosswind. To produce a slip, the ailerons and rudder are cross-controlled.

SKID This results if you are making an uncoordinated turn with too much rudder and not enough aileron. The plane skids to the outside of the turn. The skid and slip indicator's ball will slide to the outside of the turn. The rule of thumb to fix this situation is to "step on the ball."

STALL A stall occurs when the angle of attack becomes excessive and the flow of air over the airfoil breaks down. Basically, a stalling condition means the wings can no longer support the airplane. When this happens, you go down. Usually you stall the last three inches (if you're lucky) every time you attempt a landing. Stalls are an important part of flight training. A student pilot will be trained to recognize different types of stalls and recover from them if they occur at altitude.

STICK The most popular type of control system used for experimental aircraft and most fighter aircraft. The joy stick (use your imagination) usually is mounted so it comes up between the pilot's legs. Moving the stick fore and aft operates the elevators of the aircraft and controls the pitch of the plane. Moving the stick forward lowers the nose of the plane. Moving the stick back raises the nose. Moving it to the right or left operates the ailerons and makes the plane bank (roll) to the right or left.

TAILDRAGGER A plane whose landing gear consists of two main wheels under the cabin and a small steerable wheel back by the rudder. Taildragger aircraft are becoming rare items, and taildragger instructors even rarer. I was very lucky to find Virgil (my sainted flight instructor).

TBO (Time Between Overhauls) The factory-recommended amount of engine time, in hours, that an aircraft engine accumulates before it is considered due for an overhaul. A TBO of 1500 to 2000 hours is standard for most aircraft engines today.

TCA (Terminal Control Area) An area of controlled airspace around a major airport. A pilot cannot enter a TCA without getting clearance from air traffic control. As of September 16, 1993, TCAs will be renamed as Class B airspace.

THREE POINT LANDING The type of landing where the main gear wheels and the tailwheel contact the ground at the same time.

THROTTLE A knob or lever akin to the accelerator pedal in a car. Pushing the throttle in as far as it will go — "firewalling" it — provides maximum power; pulling it out as far as possible gives full idle.

TOUCH-AND-GO One of the most enjoyable and challenging aspects of flying. It entails landing the aircraft and immediately taking off again. Performing repeated touch-and-goes, trying each time to make a perfect landing, is fantastic recreation!

TRANSPONDER A little black box that transmits a coded pulse or "blip" that shows up on a traffic controller's screen to indicate your position. The transponder offers controllers a way to easily recognize your plane in a clutter of other radar returns. The addition of Mode C will inform the controller of your altitude. Transponders equipped with Mode C capability are now required for flight within TCAs across the country. Aircraft without electrical systems or aircraft with inadequate electrical systems are exempt from this rule.

TRICYCLE GEAR The most popular landing gear configuration used today. The main gear is under the cabin as in the taildragger but the third wheel is located under the nose of the aircraft. Tricycle gear aircraft possess much better visibility on the ground and are much less prone to ground loop on landing. However, you can "wheel barrow" a tricycle geared plane when landing, and that could get just as exciting as a ground loop. That's when you roll the plane along on its nosewheel and the main wheels are off the ground. (Real pilots fly taildraggers!)

VASI (Visual Approach Slope Indicator) LIGHTS Two sets of lights, one about two hundred feet from the other, located beside the runway at the approach end. These lights use a split red and white lens to indicate to the pilot whether he is on the correct glide slope for landing. The basic rule of thumb is, "white over white, you're too high; red over white, you're all right; red over red, you're almost dead" (too low). Very effective and easy to learn and use.

VERTICAL FIN This non-moving control surface is what the rudder is usually attached to. It adds directional stability to the aircraft while in flight. My Nieuport doesn't have a vertical fin and has a tendency to "dog track" (hunt from side to side) in flight.

VFR (Visual Flight Rules) You must have three miles visibility and be 500 feet below clouds, 1000 feet above clouds, and have 2000 feet horizontal separation from clouds. Basically, it means you can see where you are going and can keep clear of obstructions and other aircraft.

V_{ne} (Velocity Never Exceed) The speed above which an aircraft's structural members will be overstressed. Flying an aircraft at speed higher than the placarded V_{ne} could result in structural failure of a critical component of the aircraft. In other words, the wings or tail might come off. That could ruin your whole day.

VOR (Very high frequency Omnidirectional Range) navigation system There are VOR stations scattered all over the country. With a VOR receiver, just follow the needle and sooner or later you will get there.

WAKE TURBULENCE The disturbance that a plane passing through the air leaves behind it. Large aircraft can leave a wake that will literally turn a small aircraft inside out if the pilot unwisely follows too close. Wake turbulence can linger for as long as five minutes. It's nothing to mess with.

WHEEL LANDING A type of landing, in taildraggers, where the main gear contacts the ground first and the plane is rolled down the runway on two wheels. As the speed drops, the tailwheel will slowly come down and contact the ground. The advantages of a wheel landing are better visibility from the cockpit and better directional control in a crosswind.

YOKE A wheel-like control used instead of a joy stick in most factory-built aircraft.

MEMBERS OF THE VAUNTED DAWN PATROL ANXIOUSLY SCAN THE SKIES FOR A MISSING COMRADE. FROM LEFT TO RIGHT: TOM GLAESER, DICK LEMONS, MARK PIERCE, AND ME.

MY FAVORITE FLIGHT INSTRUCTOR, VIRGIL VETTERS, INSPECTS HIS PRISTINE SWIFT.

AND MY FAVORITE FATHER, BURKE STARKS, HELPS ME COMPLETE MY NIEUPORT.

AT THIS STAGE, OUR NIEUPORTS ARE
READY FOR RIGGING. I GUESS THIS IS
WHAT YOU'D CALL A SHADE TREE OPERATION.

NOW, HERE IS A BASIC PANEL. THE AVIONICS
SUITE CONSISTS OF A 40-CHANNEL CB RADIO.

THIS WAS MY FIRST LOVE (AFTER SHARON, OF COURSE)— MY CESSNA 120, BETTER KNOWN AS "TWEETY BIRD."

AND THIS IS MY KOLB ULTRALIGHT, WHICH, WITH MY EVER-READY IMAGINATION, I HAVE NAMED "TWEETY BIRD II."

US.

Dick Starks

Dick's interest in aviation started at an early age. When he was a prattling babe, he cut his teeth on an old pitot tube that his father gave him to play with. As soon as he was old enough to walk, he learned to fly U-control model planes and remembers sitting on the garage floor in a litter of balsa shavings as he and his dad labored to put his latest crash together.

Dick started writing about flying as a lark, approaching this pursuit with his usual eagerness and zeal. His work has appeared in such magazines as *KITPLANES*, *The EAA Experimenter*, and *Homebuilt Aircraft*.

This is his first book.

Dick has retired from his teaching career and at this writing is building a 1913 German observation/reconnaissance/bomber called the Taube (Dove). His wife Sharon, also a retired teacher, is taking flying lessons, and anticipates joining the exalted ranks of the Dawn Patrol. Dick and Sharon plan to spend their retirement years participating in air shows and fly-ins around the Kansas City area.

Bob Stevens

1923 – 1994

When I first read Dick Starks' manuscript of *You Want to Build and Fly a WHAT?* I had two reactions: (1) I wanted to publish this book. (2) I wanted Bob Stevens to illustrate it.

Bob was, and is, the premier aviation cartoonist. His cartoon series "There I Was..." ran for over 25 years in *AIR FORCE* magazine. On the civilian side, his marvelously funny cartoons graced the pages of *Professional Pilot, Private Pilot,* and *KITPLANES* magazines, as well as a number of books. His honors include four Lincoln Day awards, five National Freedom Foundation honor medals, and two Pulitzer nominations.

Bob had a lot of flying experience to draw on, so to speak. After being commissioned as an Air Corps pilot in 1943, he flew nearly every WWII plane in the U.S. arsenal and later went on to clock a world speed record of 711.75 mph in an F86-A jet.

When I asked Bob to illustrate this book, he was fighting cancer and told me that he believed this would be his last professional job. I am so glad that he was willing and able to add his incomparable touch to the book, and so sorry that his prophecy turned out to be true.

Keith Connes, Publisher

We Have More For You!

If you enjoyed YOU WANT TO BUILD AND FLY A WHAT?
you'll want to check out our other books:

CHOOSING YOUR HOMEBUILT – the one you'll finish and fly!
by Kenneth Armstrong

THE GPS & NAV/COMM BUYER'S GUIDE
by Keith Connes

Plus the video
AIRCRAFT BUYING ADVICE FROM THE EXPERTS
hosted by Guy Maher

To order, or for further information, phone toll-free:
1-888-836-3910

Or visit our Web site: www.butterfieldpress.com

Dick Starks has an interesting Web site, too:
www.kcdawnpatrol.org

Butterfield Press
283 Carlo Drive
Goleta, CA 93117